The Federal Reserve's Balance Sheet and Earnings

A primer and projections

Seth Carpenter, Jane Ihrig, Elizabeth Klee, Daniel Quinn, and Alexander Boote

January 2013

Abstract

Over the past few years, the Federal Reserve's use of unconventional monetary policy tools has led it to hold a large portfolio of securities. The asset purchases are intended to put downward pressure on longer-term interest rates, but also affect the Federal Reserve's balance sheet and income. We begin with a primer on the Federal Reserve's balance sheet and income statement. Then, we present a framework for projecting Federal Reserve assets and liabilities and income through time.

The projections are based on public economic forecasts and announced Federal Open Market Committee policy principles. The projections imply that for the next several years, the Federal Reserve's balance sheet remains large by historical standards, and earnings remain high. Using the FOMC's stated exit strategy principles and the Blue Chip financial forecasts of the federal funds rate, the projections have the Federal Reserve's portfolio beginning to contract in 2015. The portfolio returns to a more normal size in early 2018 or 2019, and returns to a more normal composition a year thereafter. The projections imply that Federal Reserve remittances to the Treasury will likely decline for a time, and in some cases fall to zero. Once the portfolio is normalized, however, earnings are projected to return to their long-run trend. On net over the entire period of unconventional monetary policy actions, cumulative earnings are higher than what they likely would have been without the Federal Reserve asset purchase programs.

To illustrate the interest rate sensitivity of the portfolio and earnings, we consider scenarios where interest rates are 100 basis points higher or 100 basis points lower than in the baseline projections. With higher interest rates, earnings tend to fall a bit more and remittances to the Treasury stop for a longer period than in our baseline projections, while with lower interest rates earnings are a bit larger and remittances continue throughout the projection period. With either interest rate path, earnings follow the same general contour as in the baseline analysis.

1 Introduction

In response to the financial crisis that began in 2007 and the subsequent recession, the Federal Reserve has been employing a variety of nontraditional monetary policy tools. The use of these tools has significantly affected the size and composition of the Federal Reserve's balance sheet, as well as its earnings. [3] The Federal Reserve's actions have garnered public attention, and Federal Open Market Committee (FOMC) members have often discussed in speeches and public forums how their actions have influenced the size of the balance sheet. The expansion of the balance sheet has also prompted questions about the interest rate risk of the portfolio. Using publically available data and Federal Reserve Bank accounting conventions, we project the Federal Reserve's balance sheet and income through 2025. The projections include alternate scenarios for monetary policy in 2013 and a rough gauge of the interest rate risk of the Federal Reserve's balance sheet.

As shown in Figure 1, through 2007, the largest asset item of the Federal Reserve (reported above the horizontal axis) was Treasury securities. The largest liability item (reported below the horizontal axis) was Federal Reserve notes – that is, currency. Prior to the financial crisis, the Federal Reserve's balance sheet grew at a fairly moderate pace, with the Open Market Desk (Desk) at the Federal Reserve Bank of New York purchasing additional Treasury securities roughly on pace with the expansion of currency and Federal Reserve Bank capital.

At the start of the financial crisis, the Federal Reserve's balance sheet began to expand at a faster pace, largely because of an increase of lending through the liquidity and credit facilities that were established at that time. [4] These extensions of credit expanded the asset side of the balance sheet, while a substantial portion of the matching increase on the liability side of the

---

[3] The Federal Reserve's balance sheet is published each Thursday in the H.4.1 statistical release, available at http://www.federalreserve.gov/releases/h41/. The Federal Reserve's income statement is found in the Federal Reserve's Annual Report available at http://www.federalreserve.gov/publications/annual-report/default.htm.
[4] For a discussion of the Federal Reserve's credit and liquidity facilities, see http://www.federalreserve.gov/monetarypolicy/bst.htm.

balance sheet was in reserve balances.[5] These liquidity facilities began to wind down as the Federal Reserve's asset purchase programs started to ramp up. As a consequence of the asset programs, the Federal Reserve's System Open Market Account (SOMA) portfolio—that is, its holdings of securities—more than tripled from 2008 to today, and in December 2012 exceeded $2.6 trillion.

Associated with the substantial change in the Federal Reserve's balance sheet has been a notable change in the Federal Reserve's net earnings. The Federal Reserve generates a substantial portion of its income from the interest-earning assets held by the Federal Reserve Banks, particularly in the SOMA portfolio. Federal Reserve expenses include operating expenses necessary to carry out its responsibilities, as well as interest expense related to certain liabilities of the Federal Reserve Banks; currently, the largest interest expense stems from reserve balances. Federal Reserve income, less expenses, plus profit and loss on sales of securities, is referred to as "net income." The FOMC pursues its statutorily mandated goals of full employment and stable prices, and the resulting net income is simply a by-product of the actions taken. The Federal Reserve is statutorily required to pay dividends on capital paid in. Under Board of Governors policy, after retaining sufficient earnings to equate surplus capital to capital paid-in, the Federal Reserve Banks remit residual net income to the U.S. Treasury.

As a result of the FOMC's actions to achieve its monetary policy goals, the Federal Reserve recently has been remitting more income to the Treasury than was historically the case. As shown in Figure 2, interest income has increased notably, particularly the portion attributable to the SOMA holdings of agency MBS. Moreover, interest income has risen significantly more than interest expense and, as a result, remittances to the Treasury have grown substantially in recent years, from roughly $25 billion per year, on average, from 2001 to 2007, to almost $80 billion in 2010 and 2011, and to nearly $90 billion in 2012, as shown in Figure 3. And, although some attention has been focused on the change in the balance sheet and the potential interest

---

[5] Throughout this paper the phrase "reserve balances" will be used to denote deposits of depository institutions that are not in term deposits. This measure is reported in tables 8 and 9 of the H.4.1 statistical release as "Deposits, Other deposits held by depository institutions." This concept is slightly distinct from the concept of reserve balances reported in table 1 of the release. That concept excludes, among other items, contractual clearing balances.

rate risk that the Federal Reserve has incurred, in fact, the Federal Reserve's securities portfolio currently has an unrealized gain position of roughly $249 billion as of September 2012. [6]

This paper describes a framework for constructing projections of the Federal Reserve's balance sheet and income statement under a variety of possible scenarios. These projections are not forecasts. As will become clear, the projections depend critically on a whole host of assumptions about future monetary policy decisions, financial market developments, and other issues. The assumptions and projections of each of those factors imply a path for the balance sheet and remittances to the Treasury. These projections illustrate how the various factors that affect the balance sheet and income of the Federal Reserve do so dynamically. Of course, other assumptions are plausible, and the aim of this paper is to illustrate how one could take various assumptions to create projections.

We base our modeling on three key inputs. First, we start with the Federal Reserve's balance sheet as of October 31, 2012 and model asset programs announced through December 2012. In particular, the FOMC's December 2012 statement indicated that:

> "To support a stronger economic recovery and to help ensure that inflation, over time, is at the rate most consistent with its dual mandate, the Committee will continue purchasing additional agency mortgage-backed securities at a pace of $40 billion per month. The Committee also will purchase longer-term Treasury securities after its program to extend the average maturity of its holdings of Treasury securities is completed at the end of the year, initially at a pace of $45 billion per month. [...] The Committee will closely monitor incoming information on economic and financial developments in coming months. If the outlook for the labor market does not improve substantially, the Committee will continue its purchases of Treasury and agency mortgage-backed securities, and employ its other policy tools as appropriate, until such improvement is achieved in a context of price stability."

The program outlined in this statement is highly conditional on macroeconomic outcomes. Modeling the joint macroeconomic and monetary policy interactions is outside the scope of the present paper. However, we consider the balance sheet and income effects of three alternative additional asset purchase amounts: no additional purchases; $500 billion in additional

---

[6] The quarter-end market value of the SOMA portfolio is published in the Federal Reserve Banks Combined Quarterly Financial Reports, available at http://www.federalreserve.gov/monetarypolicy/bst_fedfinancials.htm#quarterly.

purchases in 2013 at a pace of $45 billion per month of Treasury securities and $40 billion per month of agency MBS; and $1 trillion in additional purchases in 2013 at a pace of $45 billion per month of Treasury securities and $40 billion per month of agency MBS. Because the Federal Reserve has purchased securities in 2013, the first scenario is not possible, but it nevertheless provides a good benchmark for comparing the outcomes of the different scenarios.

Second, we interpret the minutes of the June 2011 FOMC meeting to put some structure on a plausible exit strategy from monetary policy accommodation. These exit principles suggest a sequence of monetary policy actions, starting with allowing SOMA holdings to mature and roll off the portfolio. In our projections, we assume this is the first step to exit the current unconventional monetary policy accommodation. Then we assume that the FOMC begins to raise the target federal funds rate, and finally it sells SOMA assets, in order to normalize the size and composition of the balance sheet within a number of years.

Finally, we rely on the December 2012 Blue Chip Economic Indicators forecast for nominal GDP growth and interest rates. The Blue Chip Economic Indicators is a consensus forecast based on a survey of professional forecasters; we use the mean of the forecast for our selected economic variables for guidance with their projected paths. We assume that the timing of the various elements of the exit strategy is tied to the timing of the liftoff of the federal funds rate. All of these inputs are publicly available and in no way represent a forecast from the Federal Reserve or its staff.

Key findings using the assumptions noted above are the following. First, the projections yield a Federal Reserve balance sheet that remains large by historical standards for a number of years. In particular, the SOMA portfolio expands with asset purchases in 2013 and then contracts at only a slow pace through the medium term, reflecting the fact that as of December 2012, the FOMC suggested that conditions will most likely warrant keeping the federal funds rate at exceptionally low levels for some time.[7] Under the assumption of no further asset purchases in

---

[7] The December 2012 FOMC statement explicitly stated that the "Committee decided to keep the target range for the federal funds rate at 0 to 1/4 percent and currently anticipates that this exceptionally low range for the federal funds rate will be appropriate at least as long as the unemployment rate remains above 6-1/2 percent, inflation between one and two years ahead is projected to be no more than a half percentage point above the Committee's

2013, the SOMA portfolio does not return to a more normal size until early 2018. Under the assumption of an additional $1 trillion in asset purchases in 2013, the portfolio returns to a more normal size in early 2019. In either case, the composition of the portfolio does not return to normal until about a year after the size normalizes.

Second, the projections imply that remittances to the Treasury continue at a robust pace through 2015. However, when the federal funds rate increases and securities sales commence, remittances might be halted for a few years, reflecting the elevated interest expense on reserve balances and capital losses associated with sales of MBS, both of which offset the interest income from the portfolio. Federal Reserve Bank accounting rules stipulate that when income is not sufficient to cover expenses, remittances to the Treasury cease, and the Federal Reserve books a "deferred asset."[8] In the scenario with no additional purchases in 2013, the projection suggests a low level of remittances for a few years, but no deferred asset. However, larger amounts of securities purchased in 2013 increase the likelihood of a deferred asset. The projection with $1 trillion of additional purchases has a deferred asset for about 4 years, with a peak value of $45 billion. It is important to note that a deferred asset would not have any implications for the FOMC's ability to conduct monetary policy, but remittances to the Treasury would halt. That said, projections for cumulative remittances from 2009 and 2025 are projected to be at least $720 billion, or over $40 billion per year, substantially more than the roughly $25 billion per year remitted prior to the financial crisis. This longer-run perspective on remittances is important, because the remittances fluctuate substantially from year to year in our projections, with earnings being elevated in the near term and falling later as asset sales incur some realized capital losses and interest expense rises temporarily. At the end of the projection period, when the SOMA portfolio grows at its long-run trend, remittances to the

---

2 percent longer-run goal, and longer-term inflation expectations continue to be well anchored." Moreover, the statement also indicated that these thresholds were consistent with the earlier date-based guidance that suggested that exceptionally low levels of the federal funds rate were likely to be warranted at least through mid-2015.

[8] The deferred asset is subsequently realized as a reduction of future remittances to the Treasury (which are accounted for as interest on Federal Reserve notes expense). Thus, it is an asset in the sense that it embodies a future economic benefit that will be realized as a reduction of future cash outflows. If the realization of the asset is expected to occur over several years, some valuation technique, such as net present value, would be applied to measure the value of the asset. This accounting treatment is consistent with U.S. GAAP and is similar to the way that private companies report deferred loss carry forwards as an asset.

Treasury are about $45 billion per year. More broadly, the intent of the asset purchases is to stimulate economic activity and help the Federal Reserve to foster its dual objectives of maximum employment and stable prices. Chung et al. (2011) provide some estimates of the macroeconomic effect of the asset purchases, which would likely result in higher tax revenue, and this effect would likely be substantially larger than any fluctuation in remittances by the Federal Reserve.

Third, Federal Reserve earnings and remittances to the Treasury exhibit sensitivity to the forecast for interest rates. To illustrate these risks to the projections, we consider a scenario where both short-term and longer-term interest rates are 100 basis points higher than in the baseline projection. Relative to the baseline projections, under this assumption, remittances to the Treasury cease for 2 to 3 additional years, and the deferred assets peak at larger amounts. In essence, higher short-term interest rates make interest on reserves more costly, and higher long-term interest rates make selling MBS more costly. We also consider a scenario where rates are 100 basis points lower than in the baseline projection. The lower rates dampen realized losses and interest expense, and as a result, the Federal Reserve remits earnings to the Treasury throughout the projection and no deferred asset is recorded. Under any of the interest rate paths studied here, however, on net, the Federal Reserve's nontraditional policy tends to boost remittances to the Treasury over the projection period in its entirety.

The paper is organized as follows. Section 2 provides a primer on the Federal Reserve's balance sheet and accounting, including the SOMA portfolio and the Federal Reserve's income statement. Section 3 outlines the assumptions used as inputs to the projections of the balance sheet. The balance sheet and income projections are discussed in Section 4, both the projections for the three purchase options under the baseline assumption for interest rates, and the same projections with interest rate shocks that illustrate the interest rate sensitivity of the portfolio. Section 5 concludes. Two appendixes are also included. Appendix 1 provides more detail on the assumptions underlying the projections. Appendix 2 describes the method used to derive projections of future valuations and income from SOMA securities.

2 The Federal Reserve's balance sheet, income statement, and valuation of the SOMA portfolio

In this section, we review key balance sheet components in our projections, as well as the income generated from the balance sheet. We also provide some historical context for the evolution of these items. Discussion of other assets and liabilities can be found in Appendix 1.

2.1 The Federal Reserve's balance sheet

Our discussion of the Federal Reserve's balance sheet will refer to the consolidated balance sheets of the 12 individual Reserve Bank balance sheets.[9] In reality, the accounting that will be discussed below is done at the Reserve Bank level; however, for simplicity, we focus on the Federal Reserve System's aggregate balance sheet.

Like any balance sheet, the Federal Reserve has assets on one side of the balance sheet, which must equal liabilities plus capital on the other side. As shown in Table 1, at the end of 2006, total assets of the Federal Reserve were $875 billion, with the single largest asset item being the SOMA portfolio, at about $780 billion. Prior to the financial crisis, the domestic SOMA portfolio comprised only Treasury securities, of which roughly one-third were Treasury bills and two-thirds were Treasury coupon securities. On the other side of the balance sheet, the largest liability item was paper currency, or Federal Reserve Notes (FR Notes), at about $785 billion.

With the lending that took place during the financial crisis, for a time, lending of various sorts surpassed the size of the SOMA portfolio. As of December 26, 2012, however, the SOMA portfolio was again the largest asset item, and it had grown to $2.6 trillion because of the asset purchase programs. On the liability side of the balance sheet, FR Notes, at about $1.1 trillion, were no longer the largest liability item. Instead, as the FOMC increased its asset purchases, reserve balances increased correspondingly to a level about $1.5 trillion.

---

[9] The Board of Governors does not hold assets and liabilities in the same way that the Reserve Banks do. Section 10 of the Federal Reserve Act authorizes the Board to levy semiannually upon the Reserve Banks, in proportion to their capital stock and surplus, an assessment sufficient to pay its estimated expenses for the half of the year succeeding the levying of such assessment, together with any deficit carried forward from the preceding half year.

Table 1: Federal Reserve's Balance Sheet, end-2006 and present

Balance sheet end-2006 billions of $				Balance sheet December 26, 2012 billions of $			
Assets		**Liabilities**		**Assets**		**Liabilities**	
SOMA	779	Deposits of DIs	13	SOMA	2,661	Deposits of DIs	1,533
Other assets	95	FR notes	783	Other assets	248	FR notes	1,125
		Other liabilities	49			Other liabilities	198
		memo: Capital	31			memo: Capital	55

Source: H.4.1 Statistical Release

The next few subsections review the key components of the Federal Reserve's balance sheet and how they have changed.[10]

2.1.1 The SOMA portfolio: Composition, size, and maturity structure

Over most of the post-war period, the SOMA portfolio was the largest asset item on the Federal Reserve's balance sheet.[11] During that time, the SOMA portfolio essentially held Treasury securities; however, the portfolio has held other types of securities in its portfolio over its history.[12] For example, from 1971 to 1981, the Federal Reserve purchased limited quantities of agency securities; the last of these securities matured in the early 2000s, and none was purchased until 2008.[13]

Historically, the size of the SOMA portfolio—and the balance sheet more generally—reflected growth in FR Notes and Reserve Bank capital. When currency is put into circulation, it is shipped to a depository institution and that institution's account at the Federal Reserve is debited by an equivalent amount. Because currency outstanding tends to trend upward, over time currency growth would tend to reduce the amount of reserve balances in the banking system. The Federal Reserve would purchase securities in open market operations to offset this drain of reserves. On net, therefore, the growth rate of currency tended to drive the size of the

---

[10] For a description of additional components of the balance sheet, see the interactive guides to the H.4.1 tables at http://www.federalreserve.gov/monetarypolicy/bst_fedsbalancesheet.htm, or the Financial Accounting Manual at http://www.federalreserve.gov/monetarypolicy/files/bstfinaccountingmanual.pdf.

[11] For a description of the Federal Reserve's balance sheet prior to World War II, see Banking and Monetary Statistics, 1914-1941 (1943).

[12] Refer to Edwards (1997).

[13] Refer to Meltzer (2010).

balance sheet. Similarly, when a depository institution is required to subscribe to a larger amount of Federal Reserve capital or the Federal Reserve adds to its surplus account, the result would be—all else equal—a reduction in reserve balances.[14] As a result, the SOMA portfolio must increase to offset these increases as well, creating a larger balance sheet overall.

This historical pattern is illustrated in Figure 4. As can be seen, through 2007, both the SOMA portfolio and currency and capital trended upward together. When the asset programs began in late 2008 and early 2009, and continuing through the second round of purchases in 2010 and 2011, the SOMA portfolio increased markedly and at a rate that far outpaced the growth of currency and capital. With the initiation of the maturity extension program in 2011, the size of the portfolio remained roughly constant; however, as depicted in Figure 5, the weighted average maturity of Treasury securities in the SOMA portfolio increased markedly. From a longer perspective, over time, the SOMA portfolio has had a range of maturities of Treasury securities in its holdings.[15] Prior to the financial crisis, the Desk tended to purchase securities across the entire yield curve to avoid distorting the yield curve. But after the start of the financial crisis, the maturity of Treasury coupon securities in the SOMA portfolio lengthened notably, reflecting the runoff in bills to sterilize the credit and liquidity programs in 2008, and the purchase of longer-dated securities more recently.

2.1.2 Deposits of depository institutions

Deposits of depository institutions include all depository institutions' balances at the Federal Reserve that are used to satisfy reserve requirements and balances held in excess of balance requirements. Deposits of depository institutions grew dramatically through the crisis, and are currently quite elevated by historical standards. When we refer to "reserve balances," we are using the "deposits of depository institutions" concept. These deposits represent funds that depository institutions own—they are a liability of the Reserve Bank, but an asset of the depository institution. These funds are also used for payment system settlement—for example, a payment from one bank to another (or from one bank's customer to the customer of a

---

[14] As will be more fully explained later in the paper, each member bank of a Reserve Bank is required to subscribe to the capital of its district Reserve Bank in an amount equal to 6 percent of its own capital stock.
[15] In the weekly H.4.1 statistical release, in addition to the Federal Reserve's balance sheet, the maturity distribution of asset holdings is also published.

different bank) typically results in a debit to the paying bank's account and a credit to the receiving bank's account. Lending of reserve balances and payment activity result only in a movement of reserve balances from one depository institution's account at the Federal Reserve to another institution's account; the aggregate quantity is unchanged.

2.1.3 Federal Reserve Notes

Federal Reserve notes, or currency, are a liability of the Federal Reserve. As a practical matter, the quantity of currency outstanding is not determined by the Federal Reserve. Instead, when a depository institution wants to hold currency in its vault or automatic teller machines in order to meet customer needs, it requests a shipment from its Federal Reserve Bank. When that shipment is made, the depository institution's reserve account at the Reserve Bank is debited by the amount of the currency shipment. One important source of demand for U.S. currency is from overseas. Although it is impossible to know with certainty what portion of currency outstanding is outside of the United States, estimates suggest that the fraction is one half or more.[16] Prior to the financial crisis, currency was the largest liability item on the Federal Reserve's balance sheet.

2.1.4 Capital paid-in, surplus, and interest on Federal Reserve notes due to U.S. Treasury

The capital of the Reserve Banks is different than the capital of other institutions.[17] It does not represent controlling ownership as it would for a private-sector firm. Ownership of the stock is required by law, the Reserve Banks are not operated for profit, and the stock may not be sold, traded, or pledged as security for a loan. As stipulated in Section 5 of the Federal Reserve Act, each member bank of a Reserve Bank is required to subscribe to the capital of its district Reserve Bank in an amount equal to 6 percent of its own capital stock. Of this amount, half must be paid to the Federal Reserve Banks (referred to as capital paid in) and half remains subject to call by the Board of Governors. This capital paid in is a required assessment on the member banks and its size changes directly with the capital of the member banks. Also

---

[16] Refer to Judson and Porter (1996).

[17] See the *Financial Accounting Manual for Federal Reserve Banks*, which reports the accounting standards that should be followed by the Federal Reserve Banks at www.federalreserve.gov/monetarypolicy/files/bstfinaccountingmanual.pdf, page I-68.

stipulated by law is that dividends are paid at a rate of 6 percent per year. Over the past decade, reflecting increases in capital at member banks, Reserve Bank capital has grown at an average rate of almost 15 percent per year. In addition, Reserve Banks have surplus capital, which reflects withheld earnings, and Federal Reserve Bank accounting policies stipulate that the Reserve Banks withhold earnings sufficient to equate surplus capital to capital paid in. As a result, as capital of member banks grows through time, capital paid in grows in proportion. Because surplus is set equal to capital paid in, it likewise grows at the same rate as member bank capital.

One liability item is distinct from the others. As noted above, under its remittance policy the Federal Reserve remits all net income to the U.S. Treasury, after expenses and dividends and allowing for surplus to be equated to capital paid in. As those earnings accrue, they are recorded on the Federal Reserve's balance sheet as "Interest on Federal Reserve notes due to U.S. Treasury." In the event that earnings only equal the amount necessary to cover operating costs, pay dividends, and equate surplus to capital paid-in, this liability item would fall to zero because there are no earnings to remit and the payment to the Treasury would be suspended. If earnings are insufficient to cover these costs – that is, there is an operating loss in some period – then no remittance is made until earnings, through time, have been sufficient to cover that loss. The value of the earnings that need to be retained to cover this loss is called a "deferred asset" and is booked as a negative liability on the Federal Reserve's balance sheet under the line item "Interest on Federal Reserve notes due to the U.S. Treasury." As discussed above in footnote 8, it is an asset in the sense that it reflects a reduction of future liabilities to the U.S. Treasury.

One consequence of the current implementation of Federal Reserve Bank accounting policy is that the recording of a deferred asset implies that Reserve Bank capital does not decline in the event of an operating loss. From time to time, individual Reserve Banks have reported a deferred asset; however, these deferred assets were generally short-lived.[18] It has never been

---

[18] For example, as shown on the H.4.1 Statistic Release from November 3, 2011, the Federal Reserve Bank of New York recorded a large enough deferred asset so that the Federal Reserve System also did.

the case that the Federal Reserve System as a whole has suspended remittances to the Treasury for a meaningful period of time because of operating losses.

2.2 The Federal Reserve's income statement

As the Federal Reserve's balance sheet has expanded in recent years, the income derived from the balance sheet has also grown, though the key line items from the balance sheet that generated this income are the same. As shown in Table 2, net income in both 2006 and 2011 was driven by interest income from the SOMA portfolio. Despite the difference in magnitude, in both years, SOMA interest income was more than 95 percent of total income. That said, SOMA interest income grew substantially over this period as the SOMA portfolio expanded. Interest expense, on the other hand, was minimal in both years. In particular, FR notes are a large liability without an associated interest expense. And, although the Federal Reserve has paid interest on reserve balances since October 2008, this liability item has incurred little interest expense because the interest on excess reserves (IOER) rate has been at 25 basis points since December 2008. In both years, other items in the income statement were similar. In total, remittances to the Treasury were positive in both years, but much larger in 2011 because of the expanded SOMA portfolio.

Table 2: Income and expenses, 2006 and 2011

Income and expenses, 2006 billions of $				Income and expenses, 2011 billions of $			
Income		Expense		Income		Expense	
Interest income	36.8	Interest expense	1.3	Interest income	84.5	Interest expense	3.8
Other income	1.6	Other expense	3.7	Other income	0.7	Other expense	4.5
		memo: Additions/deductions, dividends, and transfers	4.3			memo: Additions/deductions, dividends, and transfers	1.5

Source: Federal Reserve Annual Report

The next few subsections review the key line items of the Federal Reserve's income statement in more detail.

2.2.1 SOMA interest income

As noted above, income on the securities held in the SOMA portfolio constitutes the vast majority of interest income. SOMA interest income primarily reflects the size of the portfolio and the weighted average coupon (WAC) of the portfolio, less any amortized net premiums paid on securities.[19] As noted above, prior to the financial crisis, the size of the portfolio increased steadily at a moderate rate. With the adoption of the asset programs, the securities portfolio expanded rapidly and now stands at a level noticeably above its longer-run trend. The WAC, as shown in Figure 6, fluctuated over time, rising and falling with the market rates and the SOMA portfolio's holdings. This pattern primarily reflects the fact that the Federal Reserve reinvests maturing Treasury securities at auction, and the coupon at auction tends to be in line with market rates. Although the asset purchase programs resulted in a significant accumulation of longer-term debt in recent years, much of it was issued in a low-interest rate environment and, therefore, the WAC of the portfolio decreased somewhat.

Putting the size of the portfolio and the WAC of the portfolio together, as shown in Figure 7, interest income climbed at a moderate pace in the years prior to the financial crisis, primarily as a result of the steady increase in the size of SOMA, which rose in line with the growth of FR notes and capital. Beginning in 2009, interest income from the portfolio rose noticeably as large scale asset purchases increased the size of the portfolio.

2.2.2 Interest expense

With the introduction of interest on reserves in the fall of 2008 and the concurrent rise in the level of reserve balances, interest expense rose. As mentioned above, the IOER rate has been 25 basis points since December 2008, and as a result, even with a substantial volume of reserve balances, interest expense from reserve balances has been low compared to interest income and was roughly $3.8 billion in 2011.

In addition to interest expense from reserve balances, there is also interest expense from reverse repurchase agreements (RRPs), mostly generated by the foreign repurchase agreement

---

[19] SOMA interest income is defined as the rate of return on the portfolio (the product of the size of the portfolio times the WAC) minus amortized net premiums. Net premiums, though important in deriving the precise value of interest income, will not be a primary driver of the contour of the projections of interest income.

(RP) pool.[20,21] Interest rates paid on the foreign RP pool are generally in line with market rates, and when reserve balances are relatively low, interest expense on the foreign RP pool can represent a large share of total interest expense.

Reverse repurchase agreements with primary dealers and other institutions and the term deposit facility (TDF) also have associated interest expense. In addition to the primary dealers, the Federal Reserve selected money market mutual funds, Federal Home Loan Mortgage Corporation (Freddie Mac), Federal National Mortgage Association (Fannie Mae), and some banks as potential counterparties for RRPs. By contrast to the RRPs, only banks are the counterparties in TDF transactions. Although the Federal Reserve has developed the capability of conducting large-scale operations in either the RRPs or TDF, neither has been used in a material size to date, and as a result, interest expense associated with these facilities has been minimal.

2.2.3 Capital gain (loss)

Under Federal Reserve accounting rules, a Federal Reserve Bank realizes gains or losses on a security only when the security is sold. At sale, we calculate the Federal Reserve's gain or loss as the market value minus the par value and unamortized net premiums on the security. Historically, the Federal Reserve did not generally sell securities, because the secular growth in currency resulted in a need for a long-term increase in securities holdings. In 2008, however, the Desk did sell some securities to offset the expansion of the balance sheet that resulted from the introduction of the liquidity facilities at the early stages of the financial crisis. In that year, the Federal Reserve realized a capital gain of roughly $3 billion because market rates had fallen, pushing up the market price of the securities sold. With the maturity extension program, the Federal Reserve has also sold securities. In 2011, these sales realized a $2.3 billion capital gain.

---

[20] Before December 13, 2002, repo transactions were conducted as matched sales-purchase transactions, where the Federal Reserve sold a security with an agreement to purchase it again at a later date. However, because matched sale-purchase transactions were accounted for as an outright sale rather than as a financing transaction the way reverse repurchase agreements are, the transactions did not result in interest expense.

[21] Every business day the Federal Reserve conducts overnight reverse repos with foreign central banks that hold dollars in their accounts at the Federal Reserve Bank of New York. These transactions are one of the services that central banks provide one another to facilitate their international operations.

2.2.4 Payment of dividends, transfers to surplus, and interest on Federal Reserve notes due to the U.S. Treasury

As noted above, member banks are required to subscribe to the capital stock of the Reserve Banks, and the Act stipulates that the Federal Reserve pay a 6 percent dividend on this capital. Under policy prescribed by the Board of Governors, excess earnings are retained as surplus capital in an amount equal to capital paid in. Before remittances to the Treasury are made dividends are paid and earnings are retained to equate surplus to capital paid in. Dividends are paid even if remittances to the Treasury would be zero. As discussed earlier, in the event that earnings fall short of the amount necessary to cover operating costs, pay dividends, and equate surplus to capital paid-in, the Federal Reserve books a liability of "interest on Federal Reserve notes due to U.S. Treasury." This line item is recorded in lieu of reducing the Reserve Bank's surplus, and represents the amount of earnings the Federal Reserve needs to accumulate before it resumes remitting residual earnings to U.S. Treasury.

2.2.5 Remittances to the Treasury

The Federal Reserve remits any earnings in excess of operating expenses and dividends to the Treasury.[22] The use of these funds is stipulated in the Federal Reserve Act, which states:

> The net earnings derived by the United States from Federal Reserve banks shall, in the discretion of the Secretary, be used to supplement the gold reserve held against outstanding United States notes, or shall be applied to the reduction of the outstanding bonded indebtedness of the United States under regulations to be prescribed by the Secretary of the Treasury.[23]

Over time, as shown earlier in Figure 3, remittances remained in a relatively small range, averaging about $25 billion in the years immediately preceding the financial crisis. During the crisis, as Federal Reserve income increased notably, so did remittances to the Treasury. Still, remittances remained a relatively small share of government receipts – dwarfed by individual income and corporate income taxes, as shown in Figure 8, and about in line with customs deposits (not shown).

---

[22] Occasionally, statutory transfers occur, which mandate that the Federal Reserve transfer a portion of its surplus to the Treasury. The last time this occurred was in 2000, when approximately $3.8 billion held in the surplus account was transferred to the Treasury.

[23] Federal Reserve Act, Section 7, Use of Earnings Transferred to the Treasury, 12 USC 290, subsection (b).

2.3   Valuation of the SOMA portfolio

There are a number of different ways to record the value of the SOMA portfolio. Reserve Bank accounting records the SOMA portfolio at par value. The par value of the portfolio, reported in line 1 of Table 3, gives the face value of the securities in the portfolio. This is the value of the portfolio reported in the weekly H.4.1 statistical release. The amortized cost of the portfolio, also called the book value of the portfolio and shown in line 3, is the par value of the portfolio plus any unamortized net premiums associated with the securities. A third valuation of the portfolio is the market value, line 4. The Federal Reserve Banks Combined Quarterly Financial Reports and the Annual Report also report the fair value (essentially the market value) of the portfolio.[24] As interest rates change, the market value of the securities in the portfolio changes. The difference between the market value and the book value is the unrealized net gain (or loss) position of the portfolio, line 5. As of the end of September 2012, the portfolio had an unrealized gain of $249 billion, reflecting a gain on each of the three types of securities holdings.[25] September 2012 is the last published information on the position of the portfolio as of the writing of this paper; however, a similar calculation is possible at any time. In particular, the Federal Reserve Bank of New York publishes the CUSIP of every security held in the SOMA portfolio. Combining these CUSIPs with market prices for the securities allows for the calculation—on any day—of the market value of the Federal Reserve's portfolio. A rough calculation of the unrealized gain or loss position of the portfolio is also possible.[26]

---

[24] The quarter-end market value of the SOMA portfolio is published in the Federal Reserve Banks Combined Quarterly Financial Reports (Unaudited), available at http://www.federalreserve.gov/monetarypolicy/bst_fedfinancials.htm#quarterly. Alternatively, the Federal Reserve Bank of New York publishes the CUSIPs of all of the securities in the Federal Reserve's portfolio. Matching these CUSIPs with current market prices allows for an estimate of the current market value of the portfolio.

[25] Importantly, even if the SOMA portfolio was in an unrealized net loss position, the ability of the Federal Reserve to implement monetary policy would not be hampered.

[26] In addition to the market price of the portfolio, the amortized cost of the portfolio is required to calculate the unrealized gain or loss position. In real time, amortized cost can be easily approximated by the par value of the portfolio, which is published weekly, and the net unamortized premiums, which are included in the weekly publication of the balance sheet and are explicitly published quarterly.

Table 3: Value of the SOMA portfolio as of September 30, 2012
($ billions)

	Treasuries	Agency Debt	Agency MBS	Total SOMA
1. Par value*	1,648	85	848	2,581
2. Net premiums	131	1	3	135
3. Amortized cost	1,779	86	851	2,716
4. Market value	1,968	92	904	2,964
5. Unrealized Gain/Loss	189	6	53	248

*Par value as of September 28, 2012 from the H.4.1 Statistical Release.
Source: Federal Reserve Banks Combined Quarterly Financial Report, September 2012.

3   Projections assumptions

In order to construct projections of the Federal Reserve's balance sheet, assumptions about many of the details of the balance sheet and its evolution must be made. The following subsections review assumptions made about key line items of the balance sheet. A detailed description of these and additional line items is found in Appendix 1.

3.1   Interest rate assumptions

To evaluate the current and future value of securities, and therefore the SOMA portfolio, assumptions must be made about the path of interest rates over the projection period. For this analysis, we rely on interest rate projections from the December 2012 Blue Chip forecast for the federal funds rate and the ten-year Treasury rate. We use the mean quarterly rates from 2012:Q4 through 2014:Q1, the annual rates from 2014 through 2018, and the 5-year average rate from 2019-2023.[27] The assumed path for the federal funds rate and the yield on the ten-year Treasury note are shown in Figure 9. The federal funds rate remains in the 0 to ¼ percent range until the first quarter of 2015. This Blue Chip forecast rises slightly earlier than in the October 2012 FOMC statement and subsequent communications by Federal Reserve officials; in other words, the Blue Chip forecast, and therefore the forecast used in this paper, is not the FOMC forecast. After that point, the rate is projected to rise and stand at 3.8 percent in 2025. The yield on the ten-year Treasury note also rises, from its current low level of 1.7 percent to 4.9 percent at the end of the projection period. These forecasts do not represent the views of

---

[27] We use the 5-year average interest rate as our value in 2024 and 2025.

the Federal Reserve or its staff. The results of the simulations presented in this paper would be different under alternative assumed paths for market interest rates.

To perform the asset valuations that will be required, however, an entire yield curve is needed. As a result, we create a yield curve at each point in time over the projection period using historical relationships between the federal funds rate, the ten-year Treasury rate and selected intermediate tenors. Asset valuation is needed, for example, to project the effect on reserves of selling MBS as envisioned in the FOMC's exit principles—when a security is sold, reserves decline by the sale (market) price of the security, not by the par value. The higher the market value of the security, the more reserves would be drained through the sale. The lower the market value, the reverse would be true. More details are provided in Appendix 2.

3.2   Near-term balance sheet assumptions

This subsection reviews our projection methodology for selected asset and liability items that are of particular interest. All elements of the balance sheet are projected, but we leave those of less interest to Appendix 1.

3.2.1   SOMA portfolio

The evolution of the SOMA portfolio is intended to be consistent with the FOMC statement on December 12, 2012. In particular, we assume:

(1) The maturity extension program (MEP), which started in September 2011, is completed at the end of 2012, as is $40 billion in MBS purchases per month;

(2) Reinvestment of principal payments from agency securities into agency MBS continues in the near term, where by "near-term," we mean the period of time between now and the beginning of an exit strategy from the current accommodative monetary policy stance.[28]

(3) Additional purchases of securities are conducted in 2013 at a pace of $45 billion per month in longer-term Treasury securities and $40 billion per month in agency MBS. As the current purchase program is open-ended and conditional on macroeconomic

---

[28] The exit strategy and other timing issues will be discussed in further detail in Section 3.3.

outcomes, we use zero, $500 billion, and $1 trillion in total purchases in 2013 to illustrate the possible balance sheet contours and income implications of the open-ended program. Of note, the $1 trillion program is in line with the median response in the October 2012 Primary Dealer survey conducted by the Desk. The purchases of Treasury securities are assumed to be in the maturity distribution announced by the Desk in conjunction with the FOMC statement on December 12, which has roughly the same net duration as in as in the maturity extension program.

Given the initial composition of the SOMA portfolio on October 31, 2012, the portfolio evolves over time. We adjust the maturity structure of holdings of Treasury securities and agency securities through time to reflect (1) through (3) and the passage of time. Moreover, the forecast for future purchases imposes the assumed constraint that SOMA holdings that any one CUSIP remain below 70 percent of the total amount outstanding in that CUSIP, as announced by the Federal Reserve Bank of New York.

Similar to the use of Blue Chip projections for interest rates, we turn to public projections for the Treasury's issuance of marketable debt. We use projections of both the amount and the maturity of Treasury issuance in order to project securities available for purchase by the Federal Reserve. We use Treasury issuance as of October 2012, and from that point forward, coupled with the Congressional Budget Office's January 2012 projections for total Treasury debt outstanding, we generate the level and maturity structure of marketable debt outstanding.[29] In addition, we assume that the average maturity of Treasury debt outstanding extends from its current level of 62 months to 70 months by 2015, roughly consistent with the Treasury's stated intentions as of November 2011 and August 2012.[30] Therefore, future Treasury purchases are associated with coupons that evolve over time reflecting projections in interest rates, Treasury issuance, and the 70 percent ownership rule.

---

[29] As of January 2013, the budget measures agreed to so far as part of the American Taxpayer Relief Act of 2012 would likely not materially affect our projections. Other measures that could be adopted later in the spring of 2013 are difficult to forecast and beyond the scope of this paper.

[30] Refer to http://www.treasury.gov/press-center/press-releases/Pages/tg1665.aspx and http://www.treasury.gov/press-center/press-releases/Pages/tg1349.aspx.

A couple of particulars regarding Federal Reserve accounting and valuation of securities should be noted. Specifically, Federal Reserve accounting records the securities holdings at face value and records any unamortized premium or discount in the "other assets" category. Consequently, we must project both the face value of the portfolio and the associated premiums. To project premiums on future securities purchases we need to calculate the market value of securities in the future. We take the market value for securities as the present discounted cash flow of these securities using the coupon rate to generate cash flows and the yield curves described in Section 3.1 and Appendix 2 to discount these cash flows. The premium is the difference between the face value and the market value of the security. Treasury securities that are rolled over at auction are assumed to be purchased at par, and therefore have no premium.

For MBS reinvestment, we need to project the coupon of the securities that will be purchased. The model used for that is described in Appendix 2. Because reinvestments are assumed to continue only in the near term, we assume that purchases of MBS take place at a price 4 percent above face value, consistent with recent MBS reinvestment activity.

3.2.2 Liabilities and capital

In our modeling, two items are important exogenous drivers of the balance sheet contour – FR notes and capital paid in. For simplicity, we assume that FR notes grow in line with the Blue Chip forecast for nominal GDP. Capital paid in is assumed to grow at its decade average of 15 percent per year, and surplus is equated to capital paid in. This growth rate plays a role in the long-run trend growth rate of the SOMA portfolio.

Reserve balances, an important liability item for the Federal Reserve, are endogenous to our projections and in general calculated as the residual of assets less other liabilities less capital in the balance sheet projections. However, we assume a minimum level of $25 billion is set for reserve balances. That level is roughly consistent with the level of reserve balances observed prior to the financial crisis. Both FR Notes and capital are trending higher in these projections. To maintain reserve balances at $25 billion, we assume that the Desk begins to purchase Treasury bills. Purchases of bills continue until these securities comprise one-third of the

Federal Reserve's total Treasury security holdings – as noted above, about the average proportion of Treasury holdings prior to the crisis. Once this proportion of bills is reached, we assume that the Desk buys coupon securities in addition to bills to maintain an approximate composition of the portfolio of one-third bills and two-thirds coupon securities.

3.3   Exit strategy assumptions for the balance sheet

For the near-term projections, we note that the FOMC completed the MEP and $40 billion in MBS purchases in December 2012, and assume the FOMC begins one of the three purchase scenarios ($0, $500 billion, or $1 trillion) in 2013. Further out in the projection period, we base our projections on the general principles for the exit strategy that the FOMC outlined in the minutes of the June 2011 FOMC meeting.[31] The Committee stated that it intended to take the following steps in the following order:

(1) Cease reinvesting some or all payments of principal on the securities holdings in the SOMA;

(2) Modify forward guidance on the path of the federal funds rate and initiate temporary reserve-draining operations aimed at supporting the implementation of an increase in the federal funds rate when appropriate;

(3) Raise the target federal funds rate;

(4) Sell agency securities over a period of three to five years; and

(5) Once sales begin, normalize the size of the balance sheet over two to three years.

These principles represent a rough guide to the exit strategy. In particular, at that time, the Committee stated that is prepared to make adjustments to its exit strategy if necessary in light of economic and financial developments.

To complete the projections, however, we need to make additional assumptions. We tie changes in the SOMA portfolio to the date the federal funds rises from its effective lower bound, which, based on the Blue Chip forecasts, we assume is March 2015. We assume that the reinvestment of securities ends six months before this date. We do not explicitly model the

---

[31] Minutes of the Federal Open Market Committee, June 21-22, 2011, available at
http://www.federalreserve.gov/monetarypolicy/files/fomcminutes20110622.pdf.

use of reserve-draining tools.[32] We assume that sales of agency securities begin six months after the federal funds rate begins to rise and that the balance sheet has returned to normal size over about three years. In interpreting "normal size" we rely on the $25 billion minimum level for reserve balances as "normal." We summarize the assumed exit strategy in Table 4.[33]

Table 4: Key assumptions used in balance sheet projections

Assumption	$0 2013 Purchases	$500bn 2013 Purchases	$1tr 2013 Purchases
MEP Treasury Purchases			
Amount	$667 billion	$667 billion	$667 billion
Length	15 months	15 months	15 months
First month	Oct-11	Oct-11	Oct-11
Last month	Dec-12	Dec-12	Dec-12
MEP Treasury Sales or Redemptions			
Amount	$667 billion	$667 billion	$667 billion
Length	15 months	15 months	15 months
First month	Oct-11	Oct-11	Oct-11
Last month	Dec-12	Dec-12	Dec-12
Current Portfolio Strategy			
Agency reinvestments	Agency MBS	Agency MBS	Agency MBS
2013 Treasury and MBS Purchases			
Amount	N/A	$500 billion	$1 trillion
Length	N/A	6 months	12 months
First month	N/A	Jan-13	Jan-13
Last month	N/A	Jun-13	Dec-13
MBS purchase pace	N/A	$40bn/month	$40bn/month
Treasury purchase pace	N/A	$45bn/month	$45bn/month
Exit Strategy			
Fed Funds liftoff	Mar-15	Mar-15	Mar-15
Redemptions start	Sept-14	Sept-14	Sept-14
Agency sales			
Sales start	Sept-15	Sept-15	Sept-15
Sales end	Aug-19	Aug-19	Aug-19

---

[32] If term deposits or reverse repurchase agreements were used to drain reserves prior to raising the federal funds rate, the composition of liabilities would change: Reserve balances would fall as term deposits and reverse repurchase agreements rose. Presumably, these draining tools would be wound down as the balance sheet returned to its steady state growth path, so that the projected path for SOMA holdings presented here remains valid.

[33] If the expected date of the federal funds lift off is later than assumed here, the start dates for the exit strategy principles will similarly be delayed but the contours of the projections presented here will be roughly unchanged.

Other line items on the balance sheet continue on their projected path as noted above.

3.4 Income projections assumptions

Based on projections of the size and composition of the Federal Reserve's balance sheet, a projected path for interest rates, and some other assumptions, we can calculate an implied projection for the Federal Reserve's earnings, expenses, and remittances to the Treasury. Again, the details of Reserve Bank accounting matter, but we will discuss the primary determinants, which are interest income, interest expense, capital gains or losses, and remittances to the Treasury. This section describes the key assumptions behind the income projection, while Appendix 1 provides additional details.

3.4.1 SOMA interest income

Not surprisingly, since the SOMA portfolio is the largest asset item, it generates the bulk of Federal Reserve Bank earnings. Interest income reflects the coupon payments from the SOMA portfolio's holdings of securities minus the amortization of premiums on those holdings. To create the projections of interest income, therefore, we must track the evolution of the portfolio from purchases, sales, and maturing securities. As the composition of the portfolio evolves, the coupon on the portfolio evolves. The amortization of premiums reduces interest income, so the assumptions about the premiums on the securities purchased affect the calculation of interest income.

Focusing on income from Treasury securities, for simplicity, we divide the SOMA portfolio holdings into "buckets" by maturity instead of analyzing each CUSIP. Specifically, we aggregate CUSIPS by month of maturity, treating all securities maturing within a given month as a single security. Based on these buckets, we calculate the WAC of the portfolio and multiply that by the holdings. Next, we subtract off amortized net premiums.

The projection of the SOMA portfolio and the associated premiums were discussed in Section 3.2.1. As of October 31, 2012, the WAC of the Treasury portfolio is known. For the projection, we separate purchases of securities from reinvestment. Purchases occur in the secondary market at projected market prices. Over time, the average coupon on Treasury securities in the secondary market evolves as existing Treasury issuance ages and projected new issuance is introduced into the market. The starting point of the coupon rates of existing Treasury securities are from the Treasury's Monthly Statement of the Public Debt as of October 31, 2012. We assume that any purchases in the secondary market in a targeted bucket have an average coupon rate equivalent to the average coupon of Treasury securities in the market with remaining maturity in this bucket. As a result, we calculate the current market value of the securities to compute the implied premium. Reinvestment of maturing securities, however, is done at auction, and we assume that newly auctioned securities are issued at par, and therefore have no premium associated with them. For reinvestment, we project future coupon rates on newly issued Treasury securities using a regression-based term structure model as outlined in Appendix 2.

For holdings of MBS, we separate MBS purchased during the first large-scale asset purchase program from November 2008 to March 2010 and the reinvestment policy through October 2012, and those projected to be reinvested and purchased in 2013 and beyond. This distinction is important because the coupons on MBS purchased under the asset program are generally higher than the current production MBS. The MBS currently held on the Federal Reserve's balance sheet have coupons that range from 2.5 to 6.5 percent. The higher coupon securities tend to have higher premiums associated with them. MBS reinvestment is assumed to take place in current-coupon securities, which have been purchased at a premium that is assumed to be 4 percent above face value.

3.4.2 Interest expense

Over much of the Federal Reserve's history, interest expense has been modest. Interest expense derives from interest-bearing liabilities, in particular the foreign reverse repurchase agreement pool and reserve balances. Over the past decade or so, the foreign repo pool has averaged roughly $50 billion and pays interest at a rate consistent with overnight repo rates. As a result, this interest expense is relatively small. As mentioned above, prior to 2008, the Federal Reserve did not have the authority to pay interest on reserve balances. Currently, although reserve balances are quite elevated, at $1.5 trillion, the IOER rate is 25 basis points at an annual rate, which implies less than $4 billion paid in interest over the course of this year.

Interest rates are projected to rise, however, and we assume that the IOER rate will be equal to the federal funds rate.[34] As a result, interest expense will rise. But, in the projections, reserve balances are projected to decline, so the net effect on interest expense depends critically on the timing of the rise in interest rates and the decline in reserve balances.

3.4.3   Capital gains or losses

Federal Reserve Bank accounting only realizes gains or losses on the SOMA portfolio if a security is sold, and historically, the Federal Reserve sold securities infrequently.[35] In 2011, MEP sales recorded a slight capital gain. In addition, prepayments on MBS result in a realization of a gain or a loss on that security based on the amount of the prepayment.[36] For these projections, we calculate capital gains (losses) as the market value of the securities being sold minus their par value and unamortized net premiums. The market value is calculated using the yield curves and discounted cash flow methodology described in Appendix 2. In determining the Federal Reserve's income in a given period, after the earnings and expenses discussed above are calculated, capital gains (losses) are added.

3.4.4   Other items, dividends, transfers to surplus, and remittances to the Treasury

The various other components that contribute to net income are small and noted in Appendix 1. Two additional adjustments to net income are made before the calculation of remittances to the Treasury is complete. As noted above, the Federal Reserve is statutorily required to pay dividends to member banks. In addition, the Reserve Banks transfer funds to a surplus capital account to ensure that surplus always equals capital paid in. Remittances to the Treasury in any period are calculated as all remaining net income after these adjustments. Remittances to the Treasury, however, can never be negative. As noted above, if there is an operating loss in some period, then no remittance is made until earnings, through time, have

---

[34] This is a simplifying assumption. In the future, depending on the operating framework and other factors, the IOER rate could be above, equal, or below the federal funds rate.

[35] The assets held by the SOMA portfolio that are denominated in foreign currencies are revalued daily and, as a result, can experience gains and losses. These changes, however, are small compared to the size of the balance sheet and net income.

[36] Dollar roll transactions, which involve both a purchase and a sale of MBS can also result in realized gains or losses.

been sufficient to cover that loss. The value of the future earnings that will be retained to cover this loss is a deferred asset.

4 Projections

In this section, we begin with three options for the projection of the balance sheet: no purchases in 2013, $500 billion in purchases in 2013; and $1 trillion in purchases in 2013. These baseline scenarios provide a useful guide to how the Federal Reserve's balance sheet might evolve under a range of possible assumptions. Next, we examine a scenario where interest rates are uniformly 100 basis points higher than in the baseline after lift-off. Although this shock—particularly the parallel shift—is an unlikely outcome, we present it to show the interest rate sensitivity of the portfolio. As will be shown, the contours of the projections in the shock scenario are similar to those under baseline assumptions for interest rates, but the size of capital losses is larger, interest expense is higher, and remittances are therefore lower. Finally, we discuss a scenario where interest rates are 100 basis points lower than in the baseline after liftoff. Again, the contours of the projections are similar to the baseline, with losses and interest expense somewhat lower. We stress again that these projections are the result of the underlying assumptions made about interest rates and policy decisions and, as a result, are not forecasts themselves. The point of the analysis here is to establish a framework for such projections, and different assumptions would, in general, result in different projections.

4.1 Baseline scenarios

4.1.1 Balance sheet

Figures 10 and 11 present the projections of key balance sheet line items under our three baseline scenarios. As shown in the top left panel of Figure 10, SOMA holdings move up slightly through the end of 2012 reflecting the $40 billion per month purchases of MBS. In 2013, under with no further purchases (the solid line), the portfolio remains fairly steady at its end-2012 level.[37] With $500 billion or $1 trillion in further purchases (the blue dashed and red dotted

---

[37] There are some agency MBS purchased during 2012 that settle in 2013, causing the SOMA portfolio to increase slightly during 2013.

lines, respectively), the portfolio rises through 2013, growing at $85 billion per month. The peak size of the portfolio reflects the size of the purchase program: with no further purchases, the portfolio reaches $2.75 trillion, with $500 billion, $3.25 trillion, and with $1 trillion, $3.75 trillion. The level of reserve balances reflect the asset programs, with reserve balances topping out at $1.7 trillion, $2.2 trillion and $2.7 trillion in the zero, $500 billion, and $1 trillion asset purchase programs, respectively. After purchases end, under the assumption that the FOMC begins to allow all asset holdings to roll off the portfolio as the first step in the exit strategy, with the timing implied by the interest rate projections, SOMA holdings begin to decline. Notice that SOMA Treasury holdings, the top right panel, remain constant even when roll off begins. This fact is a result of the MEP reducing holdings of shorter-dated Treasury securities to near zero. MBS holdings, the bottom left panel, on the other hand, begin to contract. Beginning in September 2015, again consistent with our assumptions about the exit strategy, MBS sales begin, and these holdings fall to zero by August 2019. In the no further purchases scenario, the size of the balance sheet is normalized in April 2018 (32 months after sales begin), while in the $500 billion and $1 trillion purchase scenarios, normalization occurs in October 2018 (38 months) and February 2019 (42 months), respectively.[38]

The reduction in the size of the SOMA portfolio, along with the projected growth of Reserve Bank capital and FR notes, results in declines in the level of reserve balances, shown in the bottom right panel of Figure 11. As described above, we assume that reserve balances are not allowed to fall below $25 billion. Therefore, by early 2019 in all scenarios, these projections assume that the Desk again starts to reinvest maturing Treasury securities and begins purchases of Treasury securities. After this point in time, the SOMA portfolio expands in line with FR notes and capital and reserve balances remain constant – and unconventional monetary policy has essentially unwound.

---

[38] Although the timing of the normalization of the balance sheet is slightly beyond what the Committee anticipated in the exit principles, the sales window we assume could be shortened and the normalization date could fall within the window. The effect of selling over a shorter time period on income is ambiguous: while accelerated sales would tend to increase realized losses, interest expense should fall as reserves decline.

4.1.2 Income

Figure 12 shows the path of Reserve Bank net income under the three baseline scenarios. Because of the large size of the SOMA portfolio, interest income is elevated through 2015 in all scenarios, with the larger portfolios having higher interest income. As the SOMA portfolio begins to contract with the assumed steps in the exit strategy, interest income declines through mid-2018. After reserve balances reach $25 billion, Treasury purchases resume, expanding the portfolio, causing interest income to rise.

As noted above, interest expense reflects both the level of the federal funds rate and the level of reserve balances. The federal funds rate in the Blue Chip forecast begins to rise in 2015, and interest expense rises with it. However, in 2016, interest expense begins to moderate, as the decline in reserve balances more than offsets the rise in the federal funds rate.

In terms of capital gains or losses, Treasury securities sales conducted under the MEP result in a small gain because of the low level of market interest rates in 2012 and the relatively higher coupon on the securities sold.[39] During the exit strategy, however, MBS sales result in realized losses. Over the four-year sales period, September 2015 to August 2019, these losses average roughly $18 billion per year across all three scenarios. This amount may seem notable but should be compared to the cumulated earnings from the larger portfolio.

On net, remittances to the Treasury remain elevated by historical standards through 2015, but then decline. For the scenarios with additional purchases in 2013, remittances fall to zero for a number of years, reflecting some realized losses associated with sales and higher interest expense, and a deferred asset is recorded. The larger the program, the larger the sales and interest expense, and so the larger is the peak deferred asset.

For the $1 trillion purchase scenario, there is a deferred asset that lasts for four years and that peaks at $40 billion. For comparison, the surplus capital account—that is, retained earnings—is about the same size as this peak, and the average annual remittances to the Treasury over the projection period is slightly larger. Once sales are completed and the portfolio reaches its

---

[39] The vast majority of securities sold under the MEP were short-dated coupons, not bills.

steady state growth path, remittances to the Treasury rise slowly as the portfolio expands and interest income rises. Remittances in 2025 are close to $45 billion.

When comparing the cumulative remittances generated from alternate programs, the $1 trillion program, which results in the largest deferred asset, results in cumulative remittances that are roughly $60 billion below the scenario with no further purchases, or roughly $5 billion less on average per year. Of course, the overall effect on the federal government's finances is more complicated. For example, if these additional asset purchases provide meaningful economic stimulus, the increase in government revenues from faster economic growth could more than offset the reduction in remittances. Further, if the asset purchases lower interest rates, the interest expense of the federal government is lower.

As discussed above, only realized gains or losses affect the Federal Reserve's income. Nevertheless, given the large SOMA portfolio and the projected rise in interest rates, under the baseline projections, the portfolio is in an unrealized loss position beginning in 2014. This unrealized loss position continues to grow through 2017, but subsequently diminishes as the portfolio shrinks through redemptions and sales.

4.2   Higher interest rates

Policymakers have also discussed the interest rate sensitivity of the SOMA portfolio and the implications of large increases in interest rates on Federal Reserve net income.[40] To explore this possibility, as shown in Figure 9 under the higher interest rate scenario (the dashed line), the federal funds rate and ten-year Treasury yield rise at a faster pace at lift off, and after one year are 100 basis points higher than the baseline rates over the remainder of the projection period. One could imagine an increase in inflation or inflation expectations could lead to such a result; modeling this type of economic environment is beyond the scope of this paper and the shock is used solely to demonstrate in the interest rate sensitivity of the portfolio. We note,

---

[40]For example, the minutes to the December 2012 FOMC meeting highlighted that "[p]articipants also discussed the implications of continued asset purchases for the size of the Federal Reserve's balance sheet. Depending on the path for the balance sheet and interest rates, the Federal Reserve's net income and its remittances to the Treasury could be significantly affected during the period of policy normalization," available at http://www.federalreserve.gov/newsevents/press/monetary/fomcminutes20121212.pdf.

however, that this shock is broadly consistent with the ten highest interest rate projections from respondents to the Blue Chip survey. In other words, these interest rates are at the high end of market expectations, but are seen as plausible outcomes by professional forecasters. In the baseline interest rate projection, the ten-year Treasury yield rises by 2 percentage points between end-2014 and end-2016. By contrast, the 100 basis point shock implies the ten-year Treasury yield is increasing by 3 percentage points over these two years.

There are a couple of ways to put the size of this shock in perspective. To start, this size shock is above that expected by the respondents to the December 2012 Blue Chip survey with the top ten highest interest rate expectations (roughly 20 percent of the sample), and thus is probably comfortably above most market participants' interest rate projections. In addition, for a historical comparison, from 1978 to present, the standard deviation of the two-year change in the 10-year Treasury yield is 1.6 percentage points. As a result, this higher-interest rate scenario should be seen as a somewhat unlikely scenario, but not an implausible one. Of course, to the extent that inflation expectations have become better anchored through time, this increase in interest rates may be even less probable than the historical record may suggest.

The interest rate shock does not change the broad contours of the Federal Reserve's balance sheet, as shown in Figure 13. The higher interest-rate path does, however, change the income projections notably, and as a result, leads to a different path of remittances to Treasury. Broadly speaking, the higher interest-rate path reduces remittances as interest expense rises and losses on securities sales grow. In the longer-run, after the size of the balance sheet normalizes, the higher coupon rate on Treasury securities purchased to keep pace with the growth of the Federal Reserve's balance sheet actually pushes up remittances.

The specifics of the income projections with higher interest rates are shown in Figure 14. SOMA interest income remains similar to the baseline because the securities in the SOMA portfolio have already been purchased and their coupons are fixed. However, interest expense becomes greater once the federal funds rate lifts off from the lower bound because of the higher interest rate path. In addition, because sales of MBS occur when longer-term interest rates are higher than in the baseline, realized capital losses are somewhat greater. Overall, in the scenario with no additional asset purchases in 2013, the higher interest rates cause remittances to the Treasury to fall to zero and a small deferred asset is created. In the scenario with $1 trillion additional asset purchases in 2013, in the higher-interest rate scenario, the deferred asset peaks at $125 billion, substantially higher than under the baseline. Moreover, remittances to the Treasury are halted for 6½ years. This reduction in earnings in this scenario reflects the interest rate risk that the Federal Reserve is taking on with asset purchases. More purchases tend to lead to larger realized losses, and the losses are even larger under the higher-interest rate scenario. For comparison, however, in the higher-interest rate scenario, cumulative remittances are only about $45 billion lower than in the scenario without the interest rate shock. Under all scenarios, remittances to the Treasury resume by end-2022. As noted above, to the extent that the policies are effective in stimulating the economy, overall government revenues would be boosted on net, despite the somewhat higher losses at the Federal Reserve.

These outcomes, however, should be viewed in a longer-term context. Overall, average annual remittances to the Treasury even in this shock scenario remain above the average annual remittances of $25 billion recorded prior to the crisis.

4.3   Lower interest rates

Just as it is possible for rates to be higher than projected by the Blue Chip consensus forecast, rates may be lower than the consensus forecast. In order to characterize this possibility, Figure 15 displays the federal funds and 10-year Treasury yield under the assumption that the rise in rates is neither as high nor as fast as in the baseline consensus forecast, and in the long-run, rates are 1 percentage point lower than in the baseline. Possible scenarios that could produce this outcome through the medium run include a slower or weaker recovery than currently expected by market participants. Rather than rising by 200 basis points in the longer run, the 10-year yield moves up only 100 basis points, a modest level compared to longer-run averages. This path is broadly consistent with the ten lowest interest rate projections from the respondents of the Blue Chip survey.

As shown in Figure 16, and similar to the higher interest rate shock, the lower interest rate shock does not change the broad contour of the balance sheet projection. Nevertheless, the income projection and therefore remittances to the Treasury does materially change, as shown in Figure 17. In general, the lower interest rate path mitigates losses from sales of agency MBS and dampens expense from reserve balances, boosting remittances relative to the baseline to some degree. As a result, regardless of the amount of purchases in 2013, remittances to the Treasury stay positive in all years of the projection and no deferred asset is recorded on an annual basis. Mirroring the results in the higher interest rate scenarios, in the longer-run, the lower coupon rate on Treasury securities purchased to keep pace with the expansion of the balance sheet depresses remittances relative to the baseline case. However, despite the lower remittances at the end of the projection period, average annual remittances in the projection still remain well above the average annual level before the crisis.

5 Conclusion

In this paper, we have outlined the mechanics of and projections for the Federal Reserve's balance sheet and income. Under the baseline projections, derived from publicly available forecasts about the economy and public statements by the FOMC, the Federal Reserve's balance sheet is substantially larger than it had been historically for some years until contracting gradually during the expected exit period, and only returning to its long-run growth path in late 2018 or early 2019. This result, if it is expected by market participants and were to be realized in practice, would imply that unconventional monetary policy actions would be holding interest rates down, to some degree, for a number of years. The Federal Reserve's income and remittances to the Treasury are projected to remain at historically elevated levels for a few more years, reflecting the relatively high yields earned on longer-term Treasury securities and MBS. However, remittances subsequently decline for a time. Given the FOMC's stated plan to sell MBS at the time that policy accommodation is being removed, some losses are projected to be realized on those sales. Moreover, the elevated level of reserve balances is projected to lead to increasing interest expense for some time. Taken together, remittances to Treasury are projected to fall to a low level or to be halted for a few years and a deferred asset will be booked on the Federal Reserve's balance sheet. Subsequently, the Federal Reserve's income is projected to return to its longer-term trend and remittances to the Treasury rebound.

To demonstrate the interest rate risk on the portfolio, and to underscore the fact that these projections are not forecasts per se, but rather, the result of a set of assumptions, we consider how income may evolve with a 100 basis point shock upwards or downwards to the baseline interest rate paths. Overall, higher interest rates result in higher realized losses on MBS sales and higher interest expense, both of which contribute to a larger deferred asset, all else equal. On the other hand, lower interest rates generate lower realized losses and lower expense, and consequently, no deferred asset is recorded. In all of the simulations, however, looking at cumulative remittances to the Treasury over the period of the use of the balance sheet as a tool for policy suggests that Federal Reserve earnings are boosted, on net, from these actions. That result suggests that the Federal Reserve is not imposing a cost on the Treasury, but instead, however incidentally, providing additional revenues. Of course, any and all of the results are a reflection of the assumptions, and none of the assumptions used in the analysis reflect official views of the Federal Reserve. Rather, the assumptions are derived from publicly available information.

Bibliography

Board of Governors of the Federal Reserve System. 1976. Banking and Monetary Statistics, 1914-1941.

Carpenter, Seth, Ihrig, Jane, Klee, Elizabeth, Boote, Alexander, and Quinn, Daniel. 2012. "The Federal Reserve's Balance Sheet: A Primer and Projections," Finance and Economics Discussion Series no. 2012-56, Federal Reserve Board, August.

Chung, Hess, Laforte, Jean-Philippe, Reifschneider, David, and Williams, John C. 2011. "Have We Underestimated the Likelihood and Severity of Zero Lower Bound Events?" Federal Reserve Bank of San Francisco Working Paper 2011-01, January.

Edwards, Cheryl E. 1997. "Open Market Operations in the 1990s," Federal Reserve Bulletin, p. 859-874.

Federal Reserve Bank of New York. 2011. "Domestic Open Market Operations in 2010," available for download at http://www.newyorkfed.org/markets/Domestic_OMO_2010_FINAL.pdf

Garbade, Kenneth D., Partlan, John C., and Santoro, Paul J. 2004. "Recent Innovations in Treasury Cash Management," Current Issues in Economics and Finance, Federal Reserve Bank of New York, vol. 10, no. 11, November.

Gurkayank, Refet, Sack, Brian, and Wright, Jonathan. 2007. "The U.S. Treasury yield curve: 1961 to the present," Journal of Monetary Economics, p. 2291-2304, November.

Ihrig, Jane, Klee, Elizabeth, Li, Canlin, Schulte, Brett, and Wei, Min. 2012. "Expectations about the Federal Reserve's Balance Sheet and the Term Structure of Interest Rates," forthcoming Federal Reserve Finance and Economics Discussion Series paper.

Judson, Ruth, and Porter, Richard. 1996. "The Location of U.S. Currency: How Much is Abroad?", Federal Reserve Bulletin, vol. 82, p. 883-903, October.

Meltzer, Allan. 2010. A History of the Federal Reserve, Volume 2, 1951-1986, University of Chicago Press.

Rudebusch, Glenn D. 2011. "The Fed's Interest Rate Risk," Economic Letters, Federal Reserve Bank of San Francisco, April 11.

Appendix 1: Overview of selected balance sheet items and assumptions underlying the balance sheet and income projections

This appendix provides details about the forecasting procedure for each balance sheet item. Those not specifically discussed are held at their level as of October 31, 2012.

6 Balance sheet

6.1 Treasury securities

SOMA Treasury holdings are assumed to evolve through a combination of outright purchases and outright sales in the secondary market, reinvestment at auction, and maturities.

- Outright purchases for the $667 billion Maturity Extension Program (MEP) have the maturity buckets and targets announced by the Federal Reserve Bank of New York:

Maturity Extension Program purchase distribution (percent)				TIPS
	Nominal coupon securities			
6-8 years	8-10 years	10-20 years	20-30 years	
32	32	4	29	3

- Outright purchases in 2013 are simulated according to the maturity buckets and targets as announced by the Federal Reserve Bank of New York:

2013 Treasury purchases distribution (percent)						TIPS
	Nominal coupon securities					
4 - 4.75 years	4.75 - 5.75 years	5.75 - 7 years	7 - 10 years	10 - 17 years	17 - 30 years	
11	12	16	29	2	27	3

- Securities assumed to be available for purchase reflect those outstanding on the Monthly Statement of the Public Debt as of October31, 2012 as well as forecasts for future issuance. Holdings of any particular CUSIP are limited to 70 percent of the CUSIP outstanding, consistent with the Desk's current practice.
- The total par value of Treasury securities outstanding reflects the Congressional Budget Office's (CBO) projections for total debt held by the public.

- The average maturity of Treasury debt extends from its current value of 60 months to 70 months, consistent with observations made by the Treasury Borrowing Advisory Committee in November 2011 and August 2012.[41]
- The proceeds from maturing securities are reinvested at auction at rates consistent with the Blue Chip forecast for interest rates, as discussed in Appendix 2. Auction sizes are determined by the amount of total debt necessary to match CBO projections and follow a distribution determined by actual auctions through October 2012. This distribution is then altered as necessary to extend the average maturity of Treasury debt. The CBOs debt projections along with the maturity distribution of securities auctioned in October 2012 are summarized in the tables below.

Year	CBO debt held by the public ($ Billion)	Buckets	October 2012 Issuance by bucket ($ Billion)	Initial shares of issuance
2010	9,019	1 month	160	0.27
2011	10,128	3 month	128	0.22
2012	11,242	6 month	112	0.19
2013	11,945	1 year	25	0.04
2014	12,401	2 year	35	0.06
2015	12,783	3 year	32	0.05
2016	13,188	5 year	35	0.06
2017	13,509	7 year	29	0.05
2018	13,801	10 year	21	0.04
2019	14,148	30 year	13	0.02
2020	14,512			
2021	14,872			

Source: Wrightson, Auction Calendar

Source: CBO, Jan. 2012 "The Budget and Economic Outlook: Fiscal Years 2012 to 2022"

6.2   Agency securities

- The agency securities portfolio is assumed to evolve due to a combination of purchases, sales, and prepayments.

- Consistent with the FOMC's statement after the September 2011 FOMC meeting, principal payments from SOMA agency MBS and debt and are reinvested in agency MBS. We use a current coupon model to estimate the coupon on newly purchased MBS

---

[41] Refer to http://www.treasury.gov/press-center/press-releases/Pages/tg1349.aspx and http://www.treasury.gov/press-center/press-releases/Pages/tg1665.aspx.

securities based on the consensus long-run Blue Chip forecast for the 10-year Treasury rate and 30-year fixed-rate mortgage rate, reviewed in Appendix 2.

- Prepayments on settled agency MBS holdings as of October 31, 2012 are generated by applying the realized prepayment rate on the SOMA holdings of MBS from June 2010 to July 2011 (the period when there were no new holdings of MBS settling in the SOMA portfolio) on monthly holdings from September 2012 to the federal funds liftoff, in March 2015. This prepayment rate is notably faster than what would be predicted using the standard PSA prepayment model, likely a result of the historically low level of mortgage rates. After the federal funds rate lifts off, we gradually smooth the prepayment rate back to the long-run PSA model over a five year period.

- Prepayments on anticipated future purchases of agency MBS follow the long-run PSA model for the life of the security.

- Sales of agency securities begin six months after the first increase in the federal funds rate and last for four years. This timing is consistent with that laid out in the June 2011 FOMC Minutes; however, the exact timing is merely illustrative and chosen so as to be easily implementable in our projections.

- Under these assumptions, and given the maturity schedule for agency debt securities, the volume of sales necessary to reduce holdings of these securities to zero over the four year period only requires a six month period of minimal sales near the end of those four years.

6.3 Premiums and discounts

- Federal Reserve accounting records all domestic securities holdings at face value, rather than at market value. Except for the rollover of maturing Treasury securities, new purchases of securities are conducted in the open market at market prices. If a security is purchased for more than its face value, the difference between the purchase price and the face value—the premium on that security—is recorded separately as an asset on the balance sheet. Likewise, if a security is purchased for less than its face value, the difference between the purchase price and the face value—the discount on that security—is recorded as a liability on the balance sheet. Reserve balances increase by the purchase price of the security, that is, the face value plus the net premium (premiums net of discounts).

- At maturity of the security, the Federal Reserve will only receive the face value, so the premiums and discounts must be amortized over the remaining term of the security. U.S. Treasury securities and agency debt securities held by the Federal Reserve Banks are amortized linearly over the remaining term of the security. In the accounting treatment of agency MBS premiums, the amortization schedule for MBS is based on an effective yield calculation, which results in a constant rate of return during the term of the security. In the analysis that follows, however, we simplify this assumption and implement agency MBS amortization using the path of anticipated paydowns of agency MBS.

- As of year-end 2011, there were $88 billion in unamortized premiums and $1 billion in discounts associated with holdings of Treasury securities and $12 billion in unamortized premiums and $1 billion in discounts associated with holdings of agency MBS.[42] We use straight-line amortization of these premiums and discounts over the expected life of current SOMA holdings. We derive new premiums and discounts from outright Treasury purchases by using the difference between the assumed coupon of the security being purchased and the corresponding market interest rate, as given by the yield curve estimates reviewed in Appendix 2.

- We assume that agency MBS are purchased at a price 4 percent above par value, and therefore book some premiums on these asset purchases. Based on the calculations for the purchase prices of Treasury securities, we estimate that there are approximately $60 billion in premiums associated with Treasury securities purchases over the course of the Maturity Extension Program and $24 billion in premiums per $500 billion of new purchases in 2013.

6.4 Lending

- Since its inception, the Federal Reserve has had the authority to lend to depository institutions. Prior to the financial crisis, however, borrowing from the Federal Reserve tended to be quite small, typically less than a couple hundred million dollars outstanding per day. During the financial crisis, lending by the Reserve Banks grew significantly, at one point exceeding $1 trillion outstanding.[43] Lending by the Federal Reserve increases reserve balances, all else equal, because in lending to a depository institution, the Reserve Bank directly credits that institution's reserve account. As a result, reserve balances rose as lending increased during the financial crisis. The loan to the institution is the corresponding asset on the Federal Reserve's balance sheet.

- We make the simplifying assumption that all discount window lending over the projection period is zero.

---

[42] Refer to the Combined Financial Statement of the Federal Reserve System, available at http://www.federalreserve.gov/monetarypolicy/bst_fedfinancials.htm.

[43] Included in this number are primary, secondary and seasonal loans; term auction credit; the primary dealer and other broker-dealer credit, credit extended to AIG, net portfolio holdings of Commercial Paper Funding Facility, and the outstanding principal amount of loans extended by the Federal Reserve Bank of New York to Maiden Lane, Maiden Lane II, and Maiden Lane III.

6.5   TALF LLC

- Assets held by TALF LLC consist of investments of commitment fees collected by the LLC and the U.S. Treasury's initial funding. In this projection, the LLC does not purchase any asset-backed securities received by the Federal Reserve Bank of New York in connection with a decision of a borrower not to repay a TALF loan.
- The assets held by TALF LLC remain near their current level of less than $1.0 billion through 2014 before declining to zero the following year.

6.6   Maiden Lane LLC

- The assets held by Maiden Lane LLC decline gradually over time and fall to zero by early 2015.

6.7   Reserve balances

- Reserve balances are the residual of assets less other liabilities less capital in the balance sheet projection. That said, a minimum level of $25 billion is set for reserve balances, roughly equivalent to the level of reserve balances before the start of the financial crisis.
- To maintain reserve balances at this level, first Treasury bills are purchased. Purchases of bills continue until these securities comprise one-third of the Federal Reserve's total Treasury security holdings–about the average level prior to the crisis. Once this level is reached, the Federal Reserve buys notes and bonds in addition to bills to maintain an approximate composition of the portfolio of one-third bills and two-thirds coupon securities. In general, increases in the level of Federal Reserve assets add reserve balances. By contrast, increases in the levels of liability items, such as Federal Reserve notes in circulation or other liabilities, or increases in the level of Reserve Bank capital, drain reserve balances.

6.8   Reverse repurchase agreements

- The Federal Reserve conducts reverse repurchase agreements (reverse repos, or RRPs) by selling securities to counterparties who sell the securities back to the Federal Reserve on a stated future date. Currently, the largest portion of outstanding reverse repos is with foreign central banks that hold dollars in their accounts at the Federal Reserve Bank of New York. Known as the "foreign RP pool," as of end-May 2012, there was a little less than $100 billion in foreign RP pool transactions outstanding on the Federal Reserve's balance sheet.
- In addition to the foreign RP pool, before the financial crisis, the Federal Reserve occasionally engaged in reverse repos with primary dealers to drain reserve balances. These transactions are conceptually distinct from the service provided by the foreign

repo pool; in particular, they are intended to be part of open market operations and therefore part of the conduct of monetary policy. Since late 2009, the Federal Reserve Bank of New York has taken steps to expand the types of counterparties for reverse repos to include entities other than primary dealers, in order to prepare for the potential need to conduct large-scale reverse repurchase agreement transactions.

6.9 Currency

- Federal Reserve notes in circulation are assumed to grow at the same rate as nominal GDP. We use the consensus Blue Chip forecasts for real GDP growth and the price level to form the forecast for nominal GDP through 2025. Because this is an annual forecast, we use the annual growth rate as the annualized quarterly growth rate for the 2nd and 3rd quarters of each year, and then interpolate growth rates for the 1st and 4th quarters of the year. The table below summarizes the Blue Chip projections for nominal GDP growth.

Year	Blue Chip nominal GDP growth forecast
2012	4.0%
2013	4.2%
2014	5.0%
2015	5.2%
2016	5.1%
2017	5.1%
2018	4.9%
2019	4.7%
2020	4.7%

Source: Blue Chip, December 2012

6.10 Reverse Repurchase Agreements (RRPs)

- The Federal Reserve conducts RRPs with foreign official accounts, international accounts, and other counterparties. The volume of RRPs that is conducted with foreign official and international accounts is assumed to stay constant at its most recent level of approximately $98 billion in May 2012. The portion that is conducted with others is assumed to stay at zero over the projection period.

6.11 Other liabilities

- Prior to 2008, the level of the TGA was fairly constant near $5 billion.[44] Since that time, however, the Treasury has maintained essentially its entire cash balance in the TGA and the TGA has been volatile, reflecting the ebbs and flows of the Treasury's cash management as borrowing and tax receipts increase the cash balance and various outflows reduce the cash balance.[45]
- For the projections, we assume that the TGA follows the recent historical pattern in the near term, and then drops to $5 billion after the lift off of the federal funds rate.
- There are a set of other liabilities that we do not discuss in detail because they are, in general, either small or not particularly relevant for the purposes of these projections. More discussion of the Federal Reserve's balance sheet is available on the Board of Governors' website.[46]

6.12 Capital

- Federal Reserve capital grows 15 percent per year, in line with the average rate of the past ten years.

6.13 Deferred Asset

- In the event that a Federal Reserve Bank's earnings fall short of the amount necessary to cover operating costs, pay dividends, and equate surplus to capital paid-in, a deferred asset will be recorded. This deferred asset is recorded in lieu of reducing the Reserve Bank's capital and is found on the liability side of the balance sheet as "Interest on Federal Reserve notes due to U.S. Treasury." This liability takes on a positive value when weekly cumulative earnings have not yet been distributed to the Treasury, while this liability takes on a negative value when earnings fall short of the expenses listed above.

7   Income

- Associated with the balance sheet projections are income items. Those items not specifically discussed are assumed to generate no income or expense.

---

[44] For a discussion of Treasury cash management during this period, refer to Garbade, Partlan and Santoro (2004).
[45] Refer to FRBNY (2011), pages 28-29.
[46] http://www.federalreserve.gov/monetarypolicy/bst_fedsbalancesheet.htm

7.1 SOMA Interest Income

- The SOMA portfolio consists of four types of securities: agency debt, agency MBS, Treasury bills, and Treasury coupon securities. SOMA interest income is defined as holdings multiplied by their rate of return less net amortization of premiums.
- The average coupon on the portfolio of current agency MBS holdings is essentially fixed at its current average coupon of 4.19 percent for simplicity. Coupons on forecasted agency MBS holdings are estimated using the current coupon model reviewed in Appendix 2. Sales and prepayments have a coupon rate reflecting the weighted share of all agency MBS securities.
- The average coupon on holdings of Treasury securities, by contrast, is not fixed. The return is affected by redemptions and purchases. Three points are relevant. First, we calculate the average coupon of the remaining stock of these securities through the projection period using CUSIP-level data. Second, securities purchased in the secondary market also affect the average coupon of the Treasury securities holdings. We assume that these outright purchases of securities have a coupon that is determined by a weighted average of the coupons on eligible Treasury securities. The weights are determined by the amount of each security that is available for purchase after accounting for self-imposed limits on SOMA holdings. Third, we assume that the Federal Reserve continues to roll over maturing Treasury securities into new securities purchased at auction in the same maturity distribution as it currently uses. The coupon for securities purchased at auction is determined by the interest rate projections.
- As noted above, premiums are linearly amortized over the expected life of the securities. In these calculations, a portion of the premium is amortized each year and, consistent with Federal Reserve accounting practices, this amortization reduces interest income.[47] Securities purchased at a discount are treated in an analogous way, and increase interest income.

7.2 Other interest income

- Other interest income items on the Federal Reserve's income statement include revenue from discount window loans and other loans. Most of the time, income from these items is small compared to that on the SOMA portfolio. However, reflecting the Federal Reserve's actions during the financial crisis, interest income from loans and other assets were notable, although still smaller than income from SOMA in 2008 and 2009, comprising between 15 and 30 percent of total interest income.

---

[47] If the security is sold, the total unamortized premium associated with the security is accounted for in the capital gain (loss) line of the income statement in these projections.

- Income from other assets is calculated using the simple formula of holdings multiplied by rate of return. The rate of return for discount window borrowing is assumed to be 50 basis points higher than the federal funds rate, consistent with the spread established in February 2010. The rate of return on TALF is calculated using the observed rate of return from January 1, 2011, to June 30, 2011, of 1.76 percent at an annual rate.[48] Other assets have rates of return consistent with their own historical rates of return.

7.3 Interest expenses

- Two primary sources of interest expense are forecasted in this model: interest expense associated with reverse repurchase agreements (RRPs) and interest paid on reserve balances. To calculate the interest expense on both reverse repos and reserve balances, the quantities of these liabilities from the balance sheet projection are multiplied by the projected federal funds rate in the appropriate time period.

7.4 Capital gain (loss)

- In this analysis, capital gains (losses) are realized due to asset sales, while unrealized capital gains (losses) are calculated for the portfolio as a whole. The analysis assumes that the quantities sold are a representative share of the total holdings unless otherwise stated, and so losses are proportional to the total loss position. Realized capital gains (losses) are defined to be the market value of the asset at the time of the sale less the par value less net premiums amortized due to sales. Unrealized capital gains are similarly defined as the market value of the remaining holdings less its par value less unamortized net premiums.
- The market value of the SOMA portfolio is obtained by estimating the present discounted cash flows of the assets held in SOMA. Adjustments are made for prepayments, purchases, and sales. The methodologies for deriving discount factors and valuing of the portfolio are described in Appendix 2.

7.5 Miscellaneous items

- We have made simplifying assumptions about other income items. In particular, non-interest income is primarily from foreign exchange transactions and from priced services. During the height of the financial crisis, when the level of the swap lines outstanding surpassed $580 billion, income from foreign exchange was close to $4

---

[48] The calculation uses the average balance of the TALF and the interest income reported in the Monthly Report on Credit and Liquidity Programs and the Balance Sheet, October 2011, p. 27.

billion. In prior years, however, income on foreign exchange was more muted. Priced services income, primarily from check and other payments processing, was also a traditional source of income for the Federal Reserve. As check processing became increasingly electronic, income from priced services declined. As a result, in our analysis, non-interest income from service income is in general small and so is set to zero in each year of the projection.

- We have also made simplifying assumptions on the remaining expense items. Specifically, based on recent observations, we assume fixed annual operating expenses of $6 billion per year. And finally, consistent with the rules outlined in the Federal Reserve Act, dividends are assumed to be 6 percent of capital paid in, and transfers to surplus occur in order to equate surplus to capital paid in.

Appendix 2: Constructing yield curves and coupons on purchased securities and valuation of the SOMA portfolio[49]

The projections for the coupon rates on Treasury securities depend on forecasts for the yield curve. We construct a zero-coupon yield curve using projections for the federal funds rate and the forecast for the 10-year Treasury yield, where these independent variables are taken from the adjusted December 2012 Blue Chip forecast for future interest rates.

We specify the relationship between a yield at tenor i and these rates using a regression:

$$y_{it} = \alpha_i + \beta_{1i} ff_t + \beta_{2i}(10 year)_t + \varepsilon_{it},$$

where y_{it} is the zero-coupon yield for maturity i at time t, α is a constant term, β_{1i} is the yield-specific coefficient on the federal funds rate, β_{2i} is the yield-specific coefficient on the 10-year rate, and ε_{it} is an error term. We evaluate this specification on historical data at the 2, 3, 4, 5, 10, 15, 20, and 30 year tenors. The historical data are yields constructed from an off-the-run Svensson-Nelson-Siegel zero-coupon yield curve, the Treasury yield curve used in production work at the Board.[50] The sample is daily data from January 3, 1994 to April 10, 2010. Standard errors are calculated using a robust sandwich procedure.

The estimated coefficients and associated R-squared statistics are displayed in the appendix table A2-1. In general, the results are in line with intuition and these two rates can explain almost all the variation in the other rates. In addition, we performed a series of robustness checks. Specifically, longer-term rates tended to exhibit cointegration with the 10 year rate, but shorter-term rates did not. Overall, the estimated coefficients and resulting yield curves presented here are broadly similar to those using a cointegrated or other type of specification.

With these estimates in hand, we then construct "initial" yield curves for each point in time in our forecast, interpolating values for tenors for which we do not explicitly estimate a model. We use these for our projected coupons on Treasury securities we purchase over the forecast period.

---

[49] Much of the methodology described in this section is attributable to Viktors Stebunovs and Ari Morse.
[50] For details, refer to Gurkaynak, Sack and Wright (2007).

An additional estimate is needed to forecast the coupon rate on future MBS purchases. This is done by estimating the statistical relationship between the Fannie Mae MBS current coupon rate, the 10-year Treasury rate, and the 30-year fixed-rate mortgage rate. We use quarterly averages of daily data from 1984Q4 to 2011Q3 to generate our parameter estimates. We use an AR(3,1,0) model to account for the autocorrelation in the error terms and the cointegration in the two series. As is evident from table A2-2, changes in the 10-year rate and 30-year fixed-rate mortgage rate are matched almost one-to-one with those in the MBS current coupon rate, and the autocorrelation in the differenced series, while not strong, is still persistent enough to be relevant in tests for autocorrelation of the residuals.

Table A2-1: Yield curve regressions

Year	Effective rate			10-year rate			Constant			R-squared
	Coefficient	Standard error	T-stat	Coefficient	Standard error	T-stat	Coefficient	Standard error	T-stat	
2	0.536***	0.003	155.438	0.746***	0.007	109.305	-0.018***	0	-62.483	0.971
3	0.392***	0.003	131.062	0.877***	0.006	154.592	-0.018***	0	-72.969	0.975
4	0.282***	0.002	116.573	0.945***	0.004	211.367	-0.015***	0	-80.671	0.982
5	0.196***	0.002	107.059	0.980***	0.003	293.544	-0.012***	0	-87.013	0.988
7	0.071***	0.001	87.829	1.003***	0.001	678.057	-0.006***	0	-95.999	0.997
10	-0.039***	0	-119.39	1.000***	0.001	1420.984	0.002***	0	59.475	0.999
15	-0.121***	0.001	-88.754	0.995***	0.003	397.277	0.008***	0	76.072	0.983
20	-0.149***	0.002	-64.611	1.013***	0.004	269.745	0.010***	0	54.576	0.953
30	-0.168***	0.004	-46.25	1.083***	0.006	196.249	0.005***	0	19.391	0.9

N: 4067

Sample: 1/3/1994-4/10/2010

Table A2-2: MBS coupon forecasting regression

Dependent variable: Δ(Fannie Mae 30-year current coupon)		
	Coefficient	Std. Error
Δ(10 year-rate)	0.235	0.051
Δ(30yr fixed-rate mortgage rate)	0.858	0.059
Constant	0.004	0.007
AR Term		
L1	-0.254	0.109
L2	-0.07	0.111
L3	-0.242	0.121

N = 107

Sample period: 1984Q4 to 2011Q3

Figure 1 – Federal Reserve's Assets and Liabilities

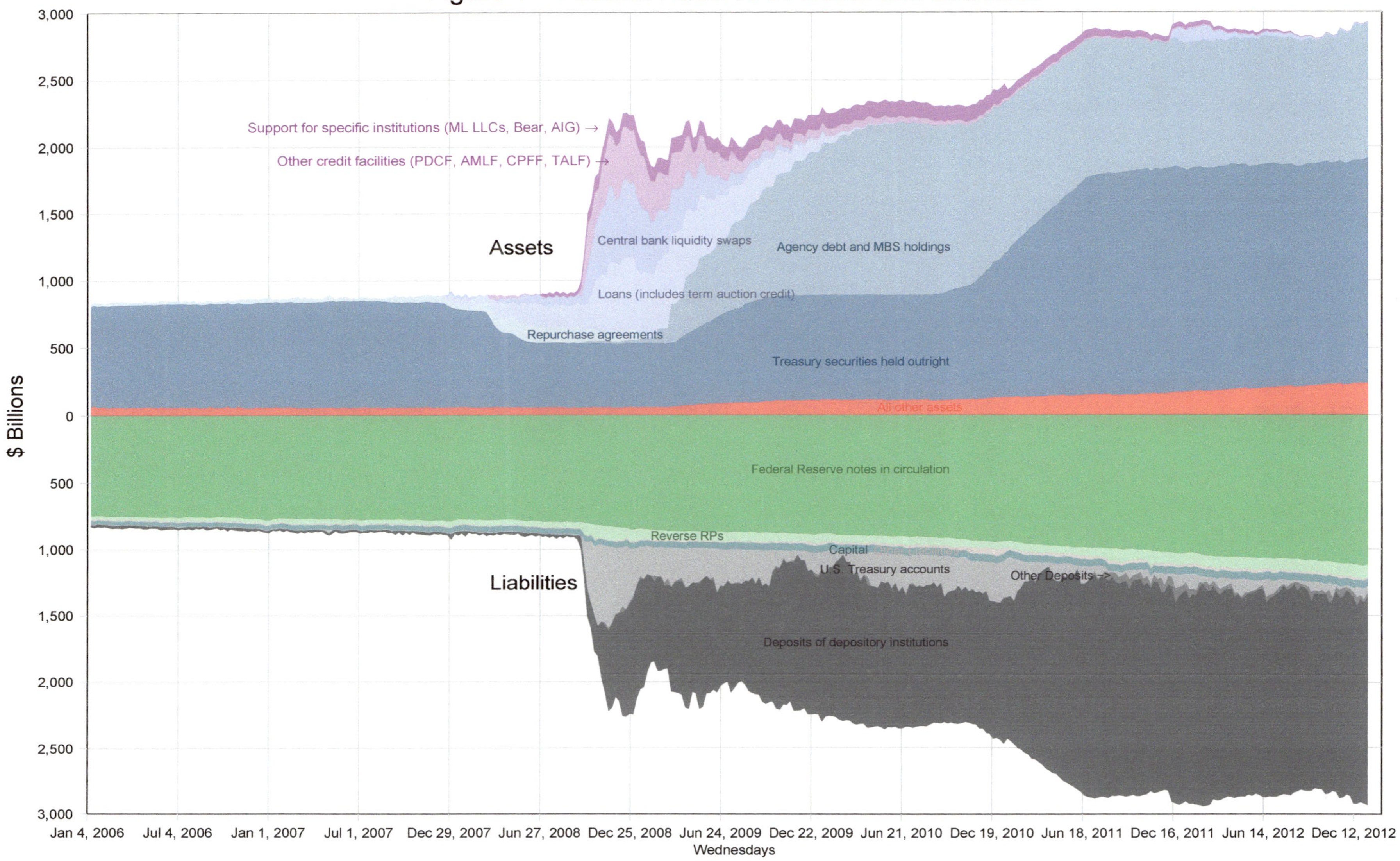

Assets

Support for specific institutions (ML LLCs, Bear, AIG) →
Other credit facilities (PDCF, AMLF, CPFF, TALF) →
Central bank liquidity swaps
Agency debt and MBS holdings
Loans (includes term auction credit)
Repurchase agreements
Treasury securities held outright
All other assets

Liabilities

Federal Reserve notes in circulation
Reverse RPs
Capital
Other Deposits →
U.S. Treasury accounts
Deposits of depository institutions

$ Billions

3,000
2,500
2,000
1,500
1,000
500
0
500
1,000
1,500
2,000
2,500
3,000

Jan 4, 2006 Jul 4, 2006 Jan 1, 2007 Jul 1, 2007 Dec 29, 2007 Jun 27, 2008 Dec 25, 2008 Jun 24, 2009 Dec 22, 2009 Jun 21, 2010 Dec 19, 2010 Jun 18, 2011 Dec 16, 2011 Jun 14, 2012 Dec 12, 2012
Wednesdays

Last updated December 26, 2012.

Source: H.4.1 Statistical Release

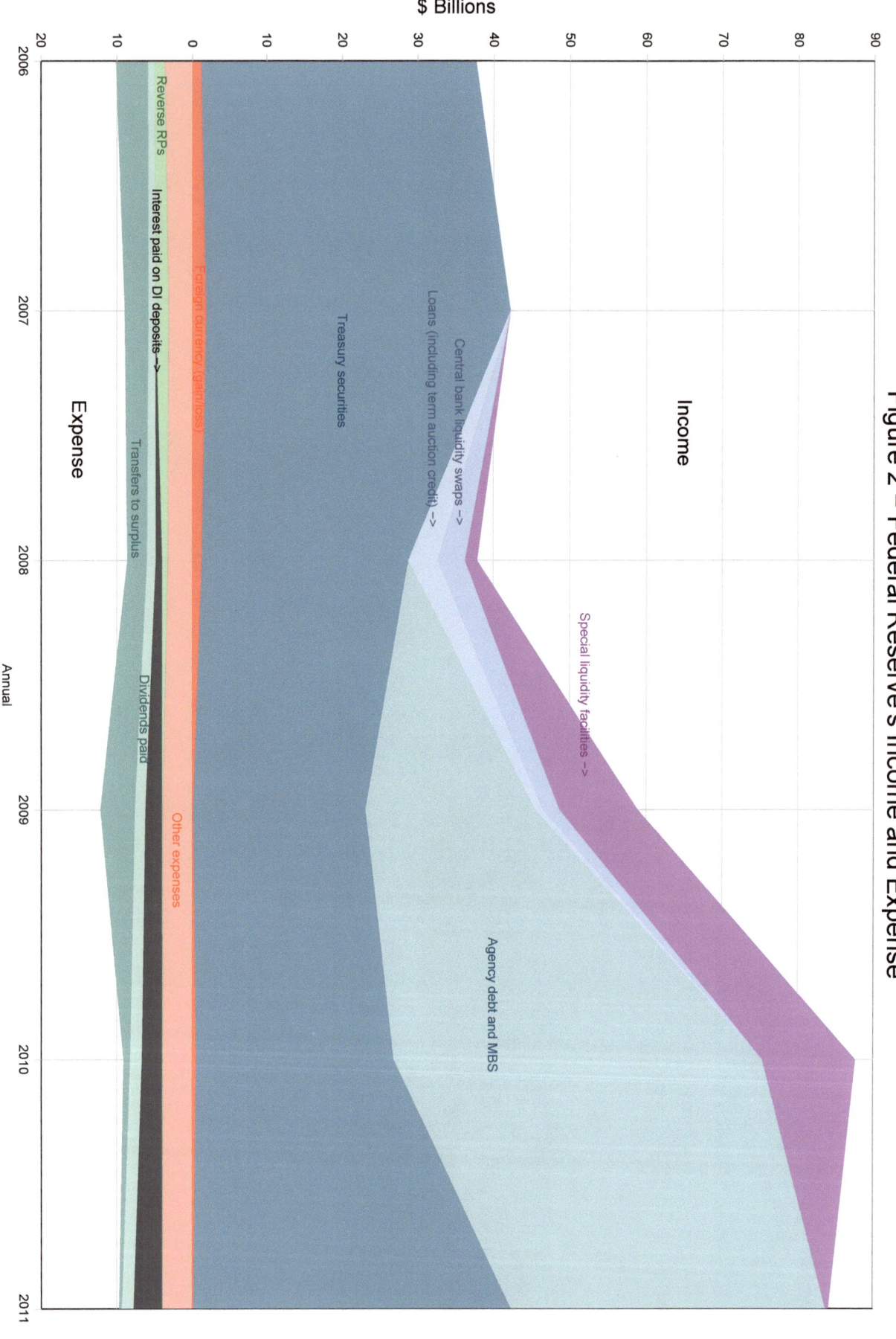

Figure 2 – Federal Reserve's Income and Expense

$ Billions

Income

Expense

Annual

Treasury securities

Loans (including term auction credit) –>

Central bank liquidity swaps –>

Special liquidity facilities –>

Agency debt and MBS

Reverse RPs

Interest paid on DI deposits –>

Transfers to surplus

Dividends paid

Foreign currency (gain/loss)

Other expenses

Source: Annual Report of the Federal Reserve Board of Governors

Figure 3 - Federal Reserve Distributions to the U.S. Treasury

$Billion

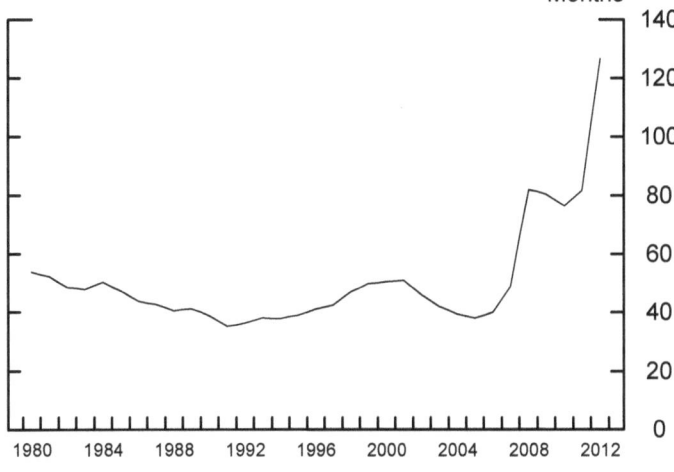

Source: Annual Report of the Federal Reserve Board of Governors;
*Preliminary unaudited estimate,
 see http://www.federalreserve.gov/newsevents/press/other/20130110a.htm

Figure 4 - SOMA, Capital + FR Notes, and Reserve Balances

$Billion

SOMA
Capital+Notes
Reserve Balances

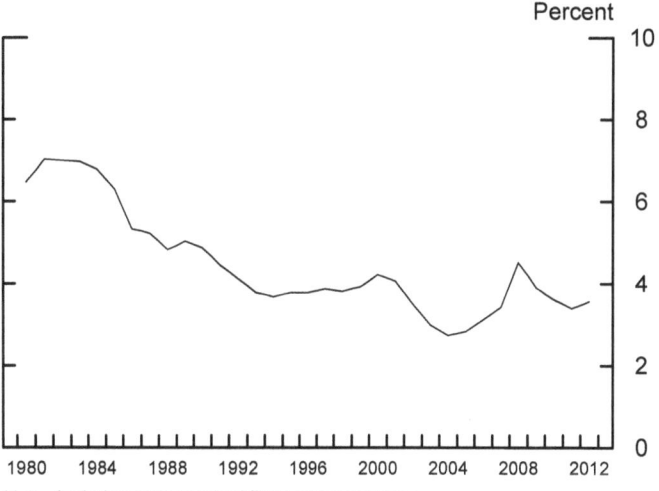

Source: H.4.1 Statistical Release

Figure 5 - Weighted Average Maturity of SOMA

Months

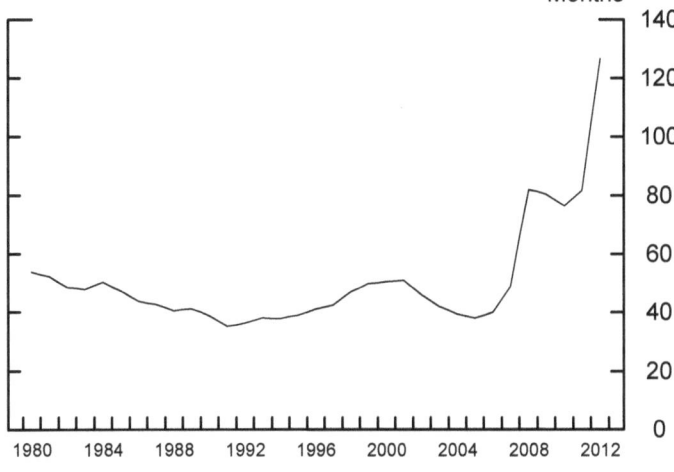

Note. Includes only nominal Treasury securities;
Source: Federal Reserve Bank of New York

Figure 6 - Weighted Average Coupon of SOMA

Percent

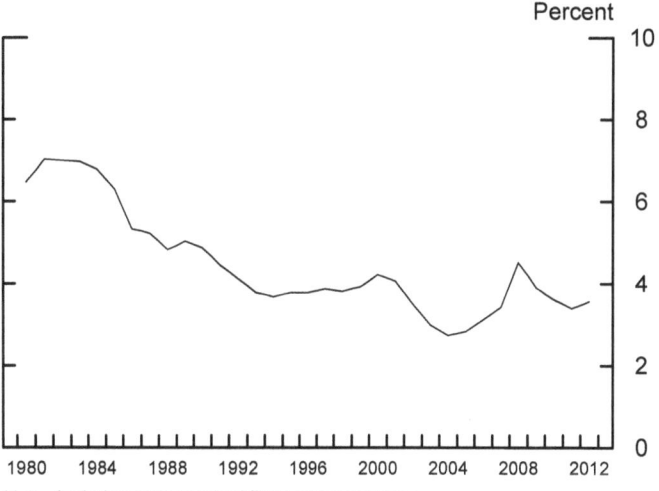

Note. Includes only nominal Treasury securities;
Source: Federal Reserve Bank of New York

Figure 7 - Interest Income

$Billion

Total Interest Income
SOMA Interest Income

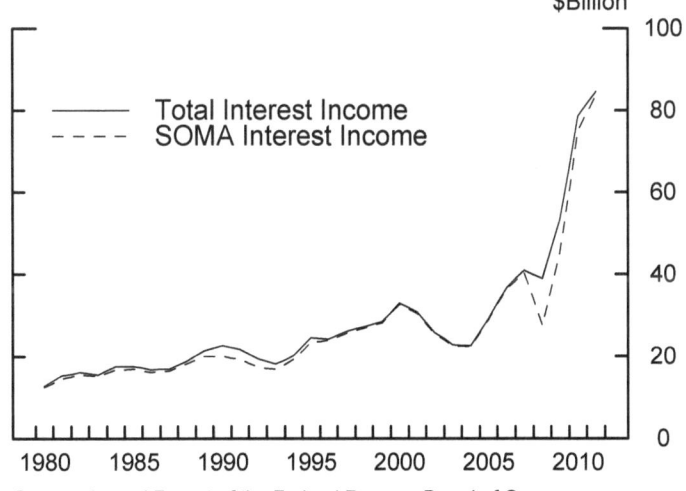

Source: Annual Report of the Federal Reserve Board of Governors

Figure 8 - Selected Treasury Receipts

$Billion

Fed Earnings
Social Security
Individual Income Taxes
Corporate Income Taxes

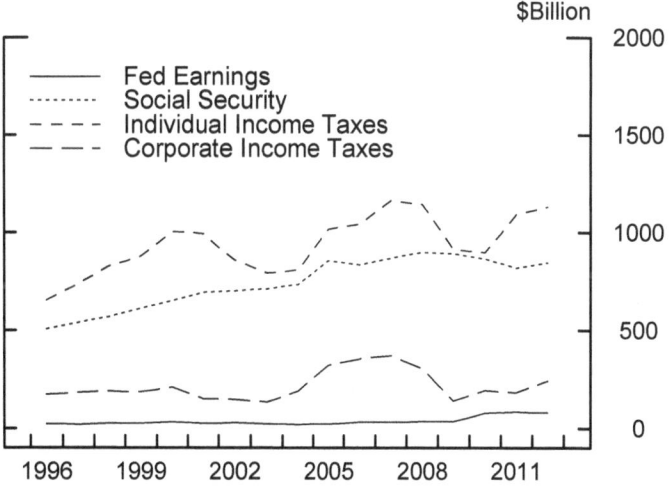

Source: United States Treasury Bulletin

Figure 9 - Interest Rates*

Federal Funds Rate

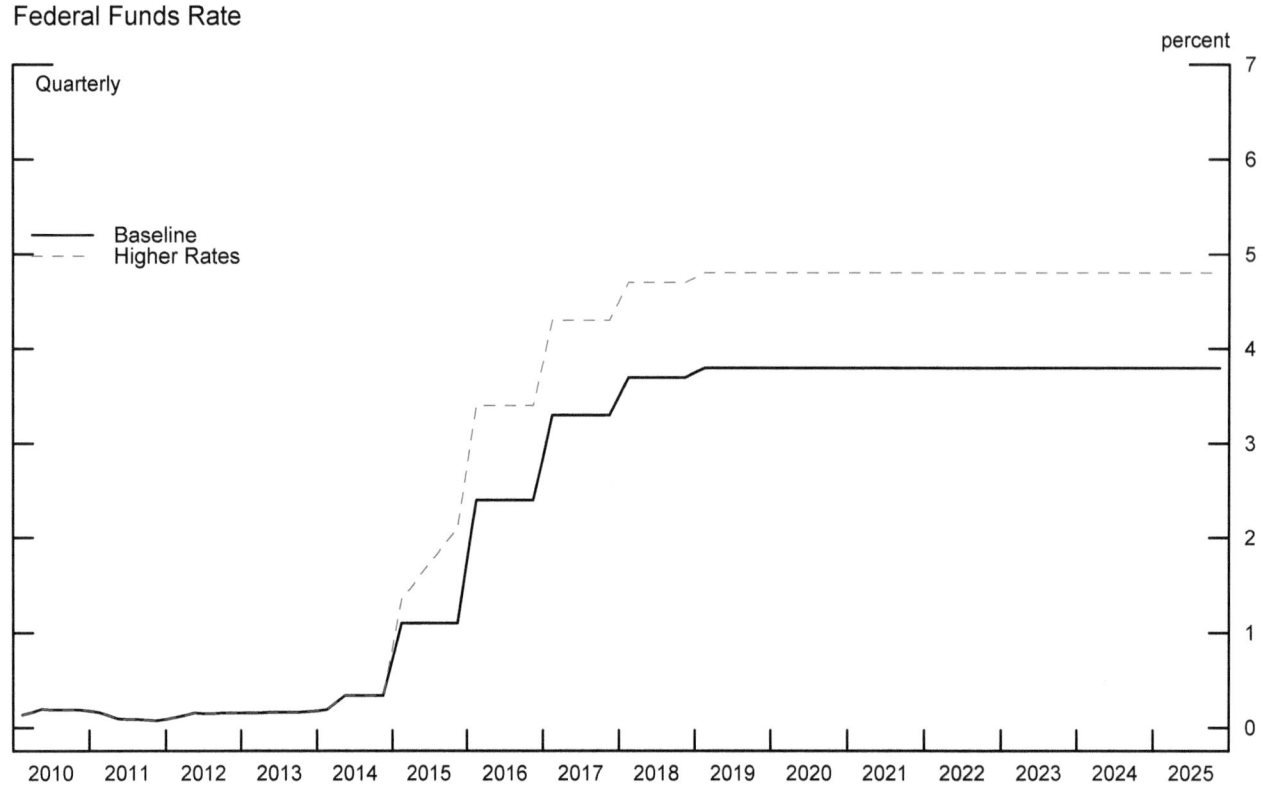

10 year Treasury Rate

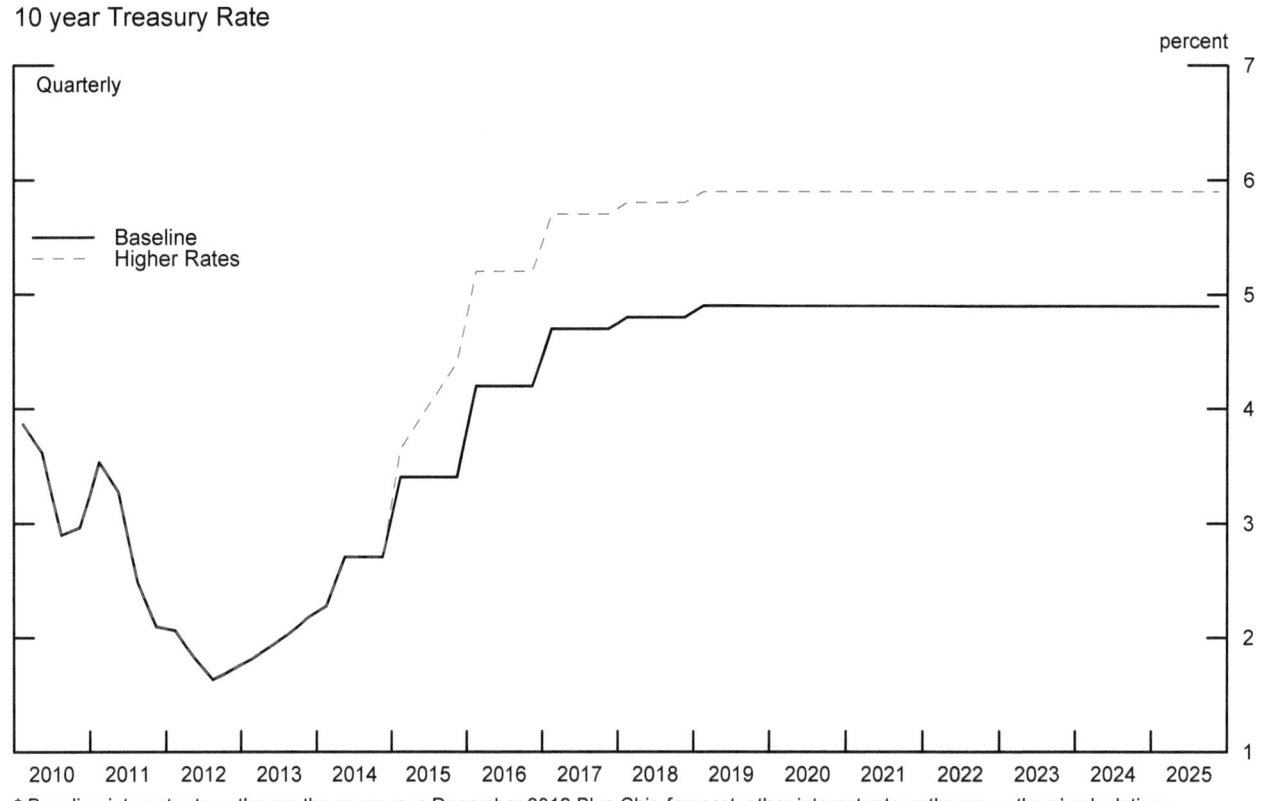

* Baseline interest rate paths are the consensus December 2012 Blue Chip forecast, other interest rate paths are authors' calculations

Figure 10 - Selected Assets Projections

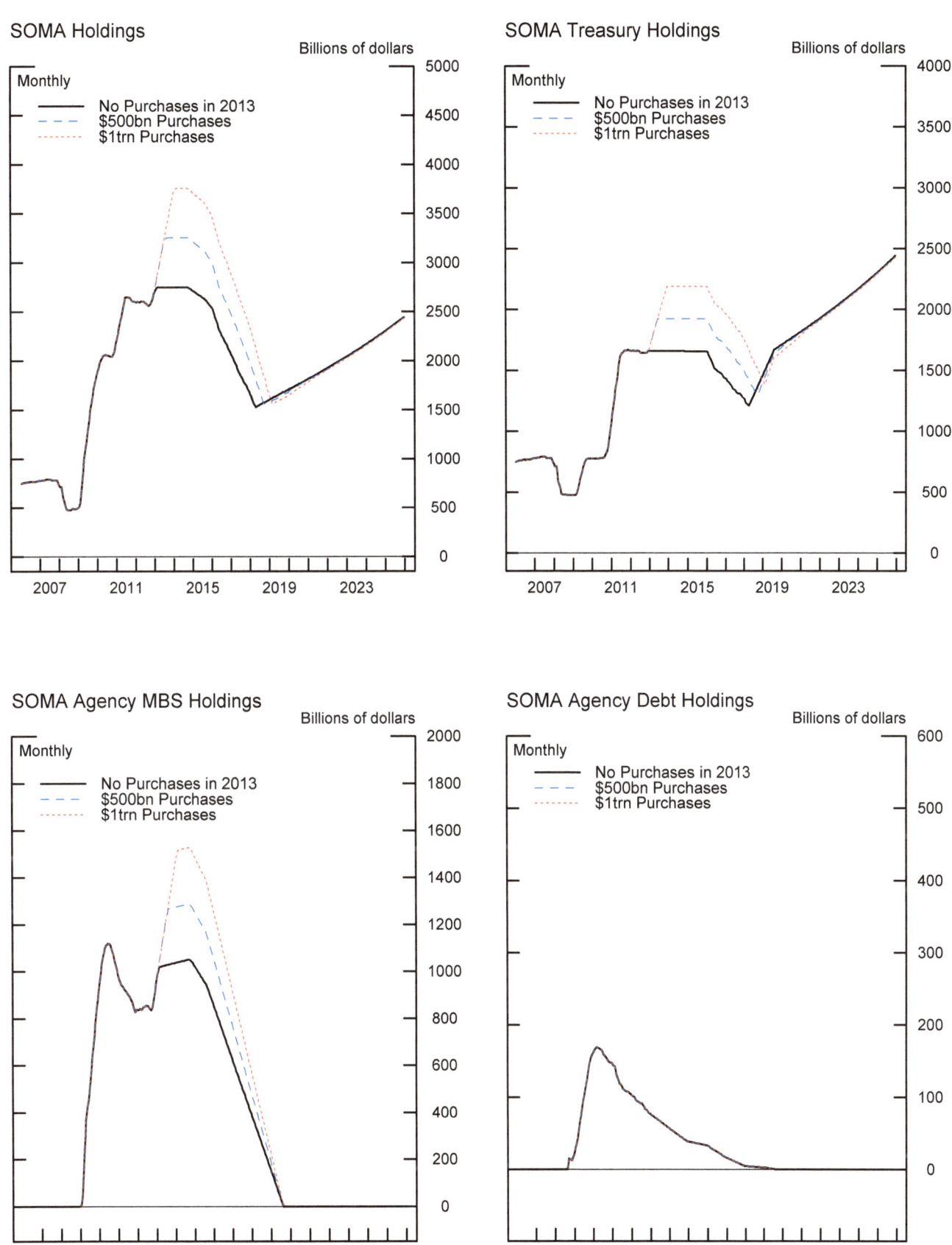

Source: Authors' Projections

Figure 11 - Selected Liabilities Projections

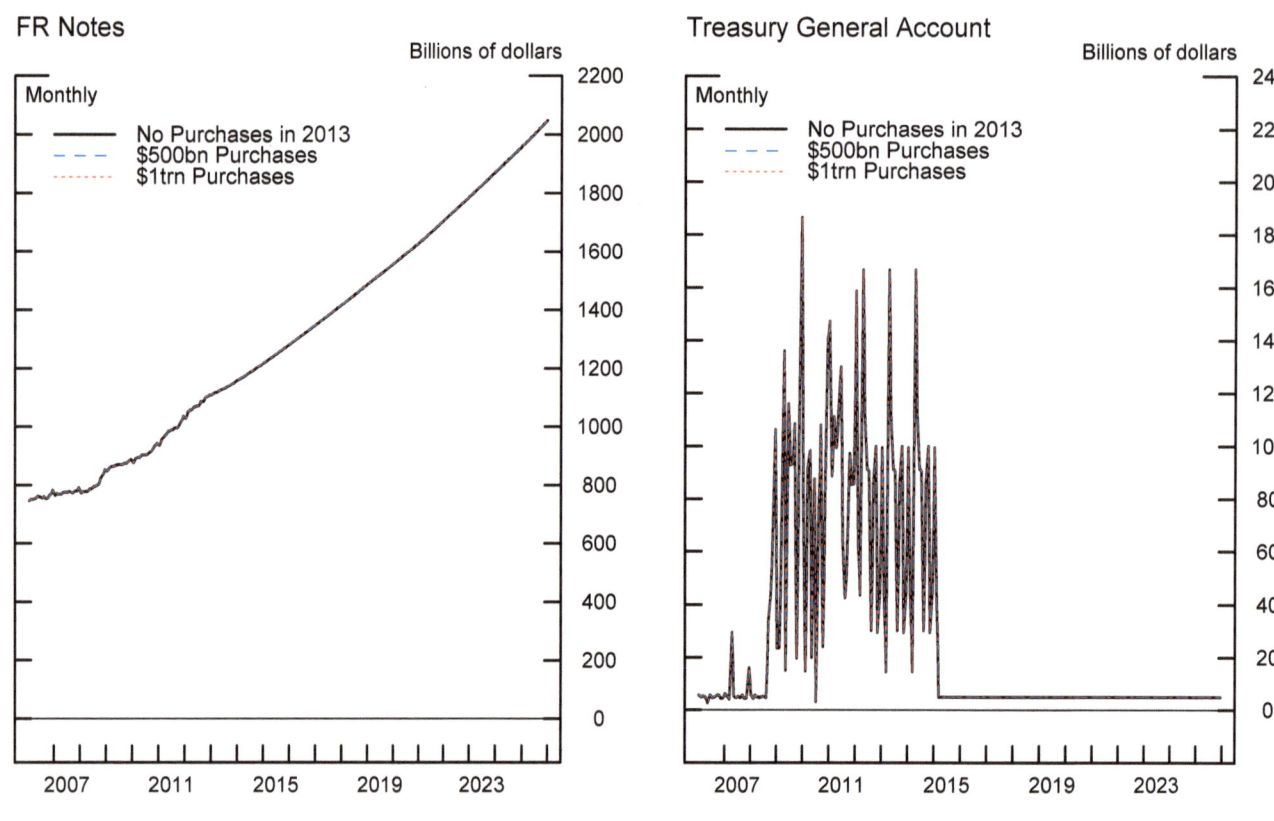

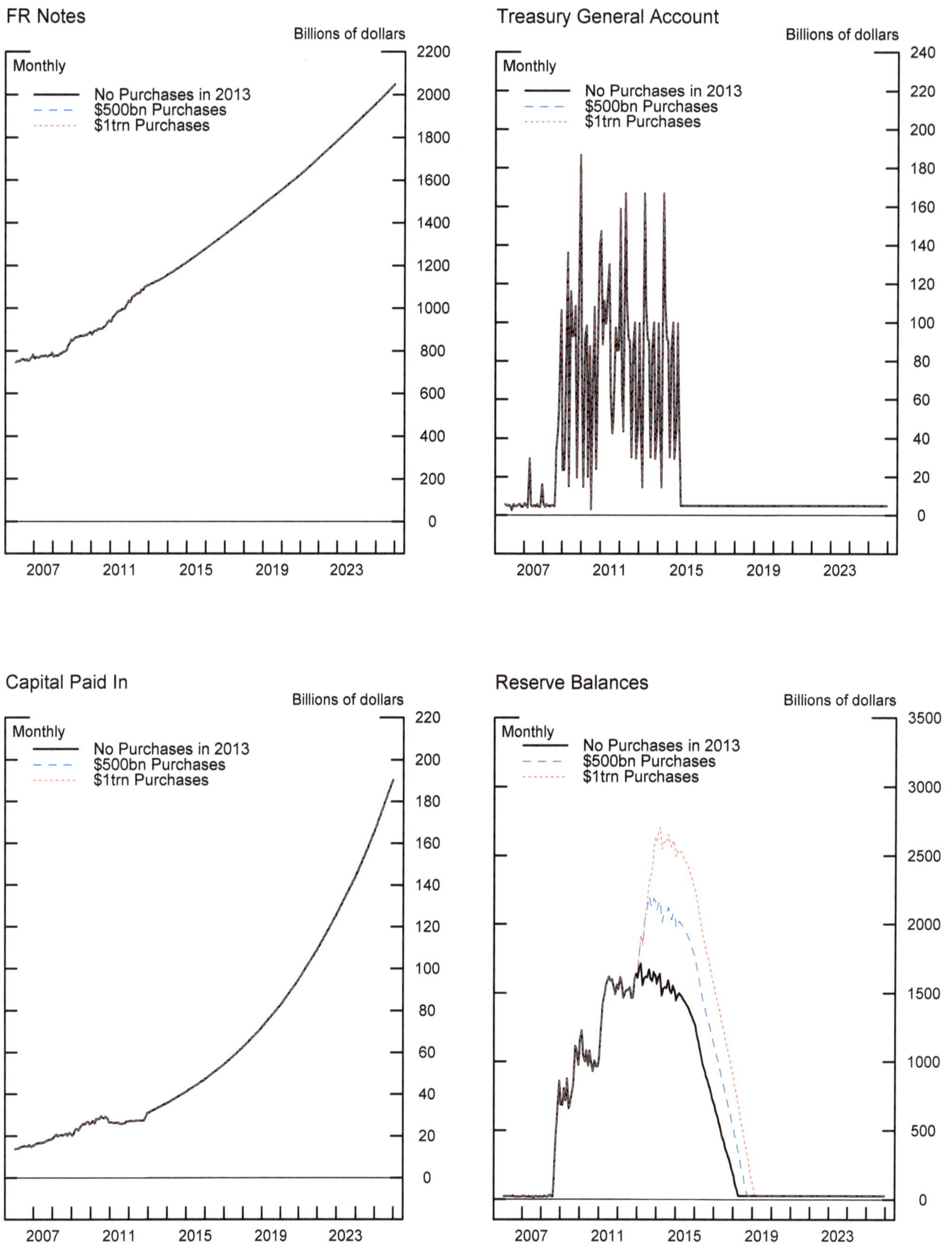

Source: Authors' Projections

Figure 12 - Income Projections

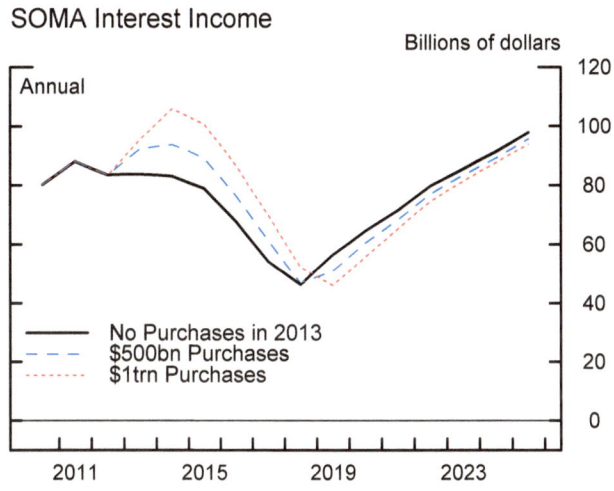

SOMA Interest Income

Billions of dollars

Annual

— No Purchases in 2013
--- $500bn Purchases
.... $1trn Purchases

120
100
80
60
40
20
0

2011   2015   2019   2023

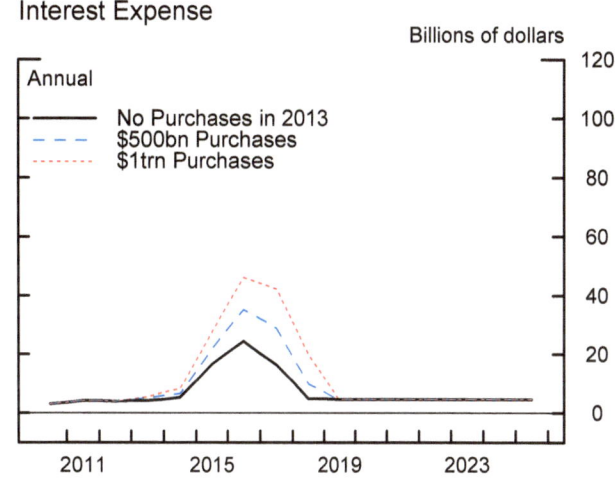

Interest Expense

Billions of dollars

Annual

— No Purchases in 2013
--- $500bn Purchases
.... $1trn Purchases

120
100
80
60
40
20
0

2011   2015   2019   2023

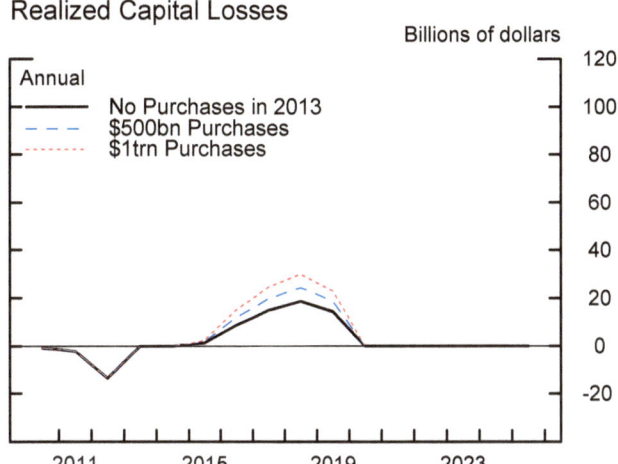

Realized Capital Losses

Billions of dollars

Annual

— No Purchases in 2013
--- $500bn Purchases
.... $1trn Purchases

120
100
80
60
40
20
0
-20

2011   2015   2019   2023

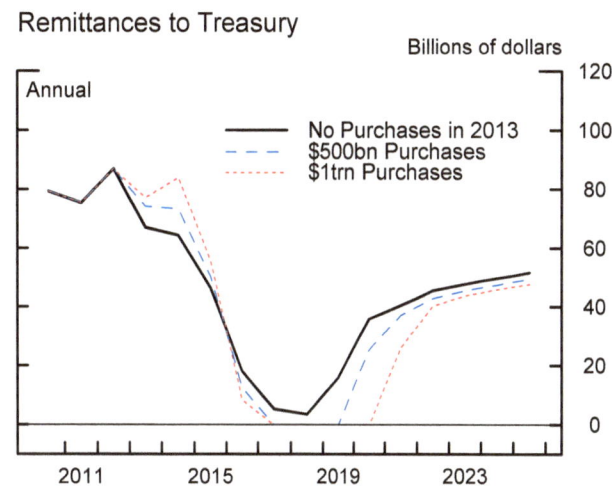

Remittances to Treasury

Billions of dollars

Annual

— No Purchases in 2013
--- $500bn Purchases
.... $1trn Purchases

120
100
80
60
40
20
0

2011   2015   2019   2023

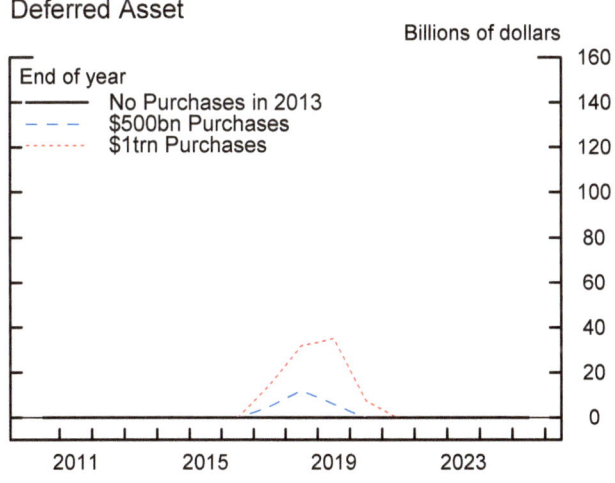

Deferred Asset

Billions of dollars

End of year

— No Purchases in 2013
--- $500bn Purchases
.... $1trn Purchases

160
140
120
100
80
60
40
20
0

2011   2015   2019   2023

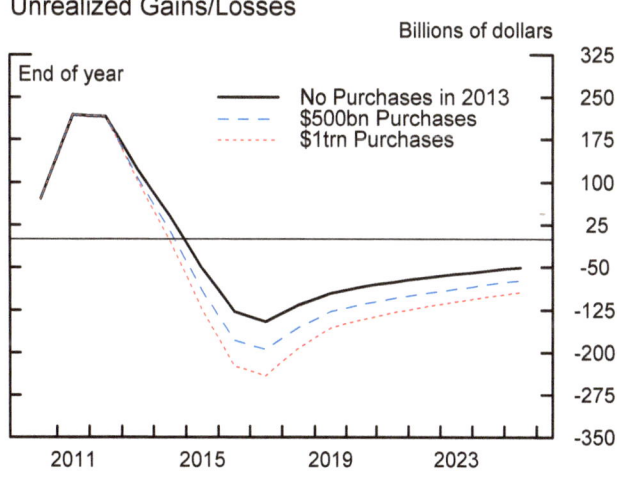

Unrealized Gains/Losses

Billions of dollars

End of year

— No Purchases in 2013
--- $500bn Purchases
.... $1trn Purchases

325
250
175
100
25
-50
-125
-200
-275
-350

2011   2015   2019   2023

Source: Authors' Projections

Figure 13 - Selected Balance Sheet Items with Higher Interest Rates

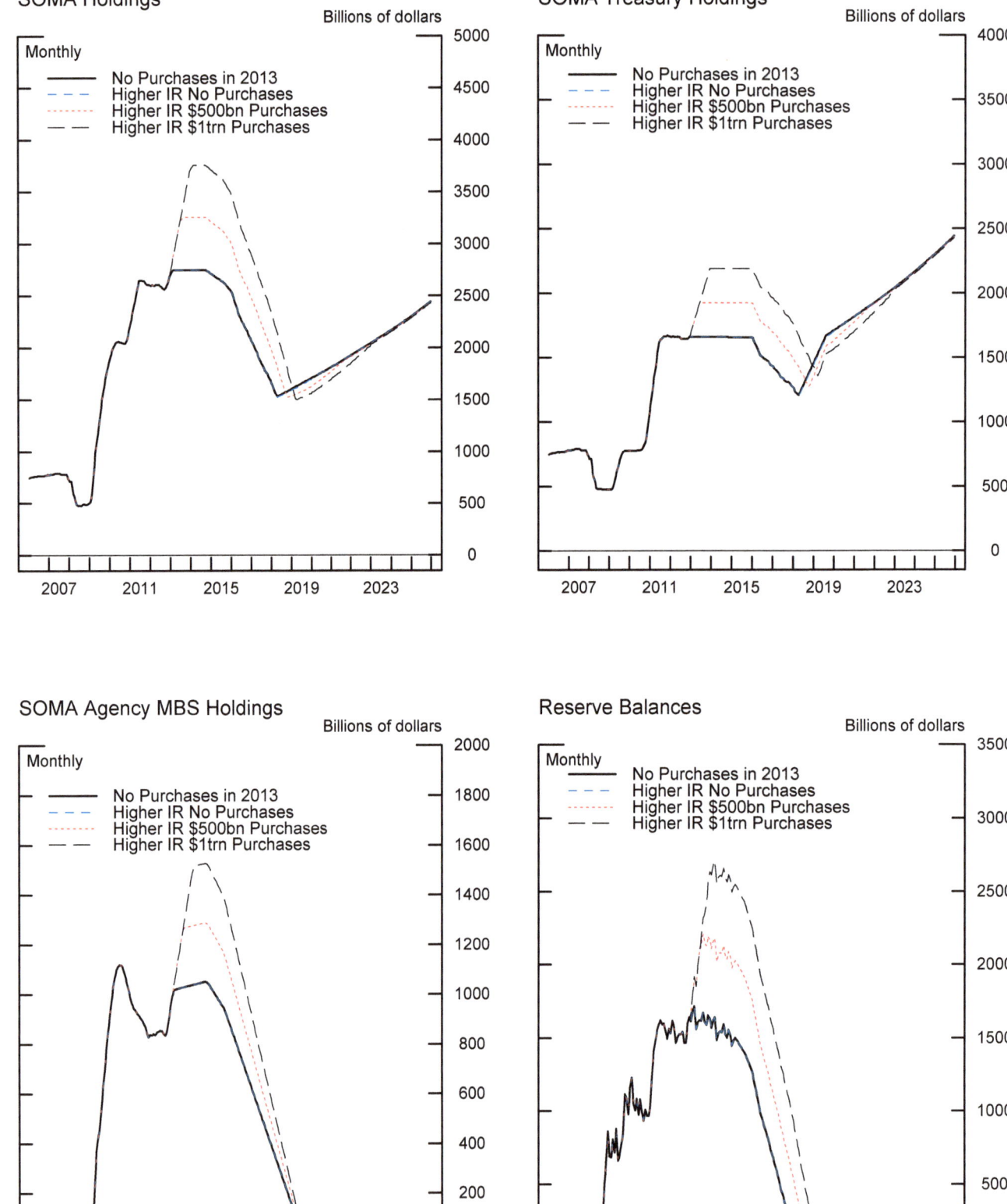

Source: Authors' Projections

Figure 14 - Income Projections with Higher Interest Rates

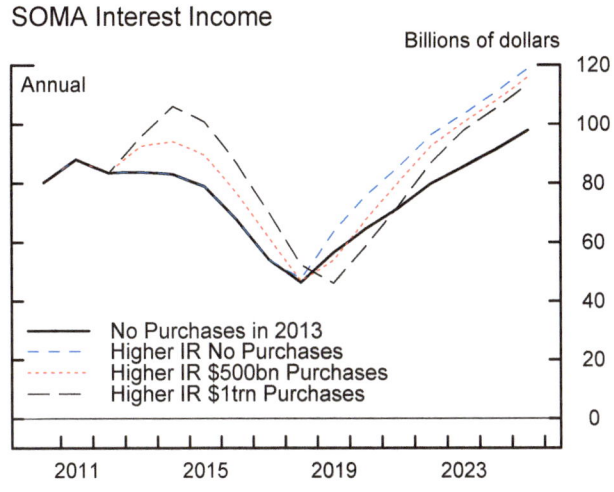

SOMA Interest Income

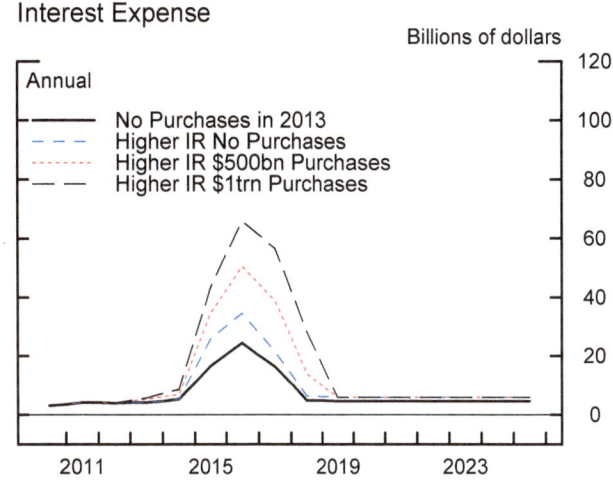

Interest Expense

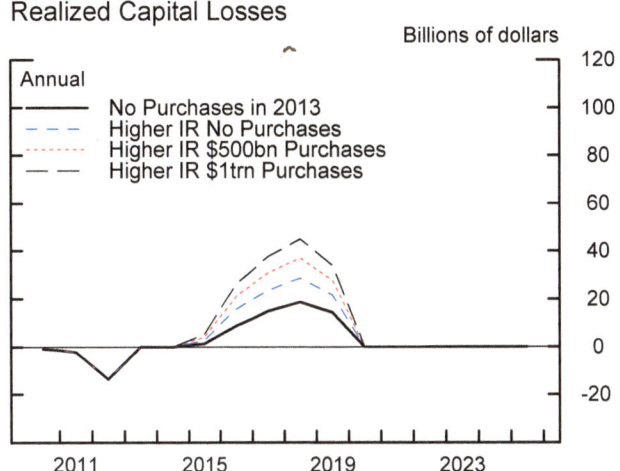

Realized Capital Losses

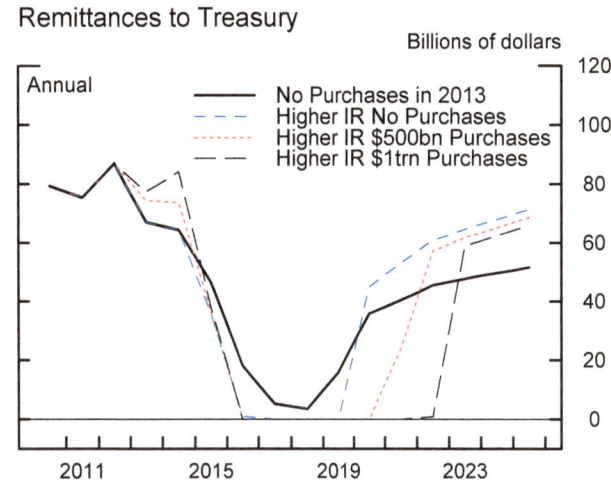

Remittances to Treasury

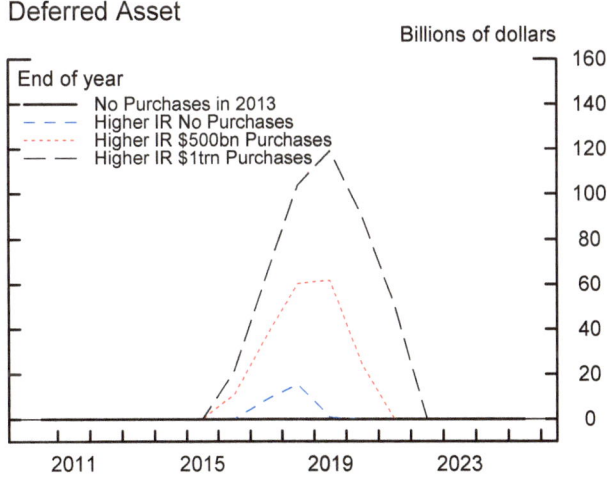

Deferred Asset

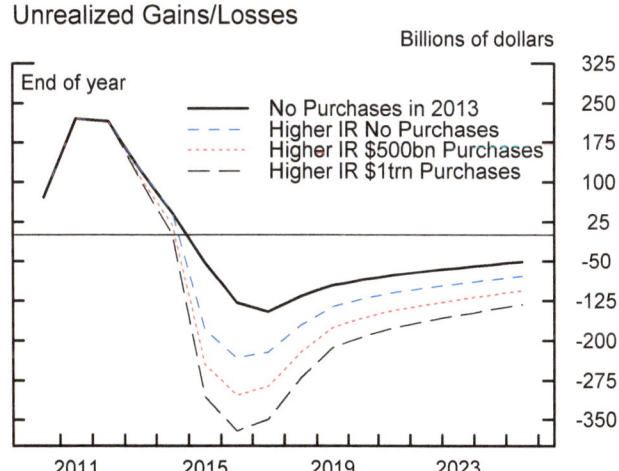

Unrealized Gains/Losses

Source: Authors' Projections

Figure 15 - Interest Rates*

Federal Funds Rate

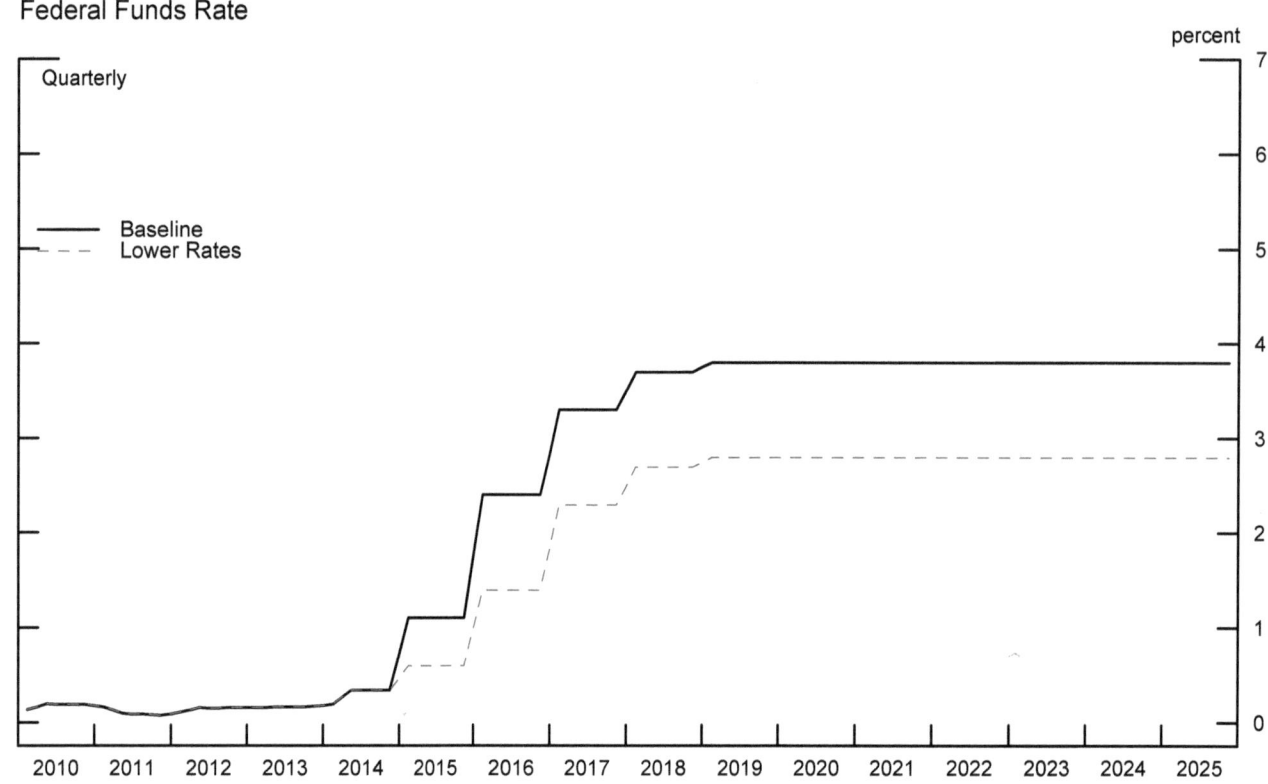

10 year Treasury Rate

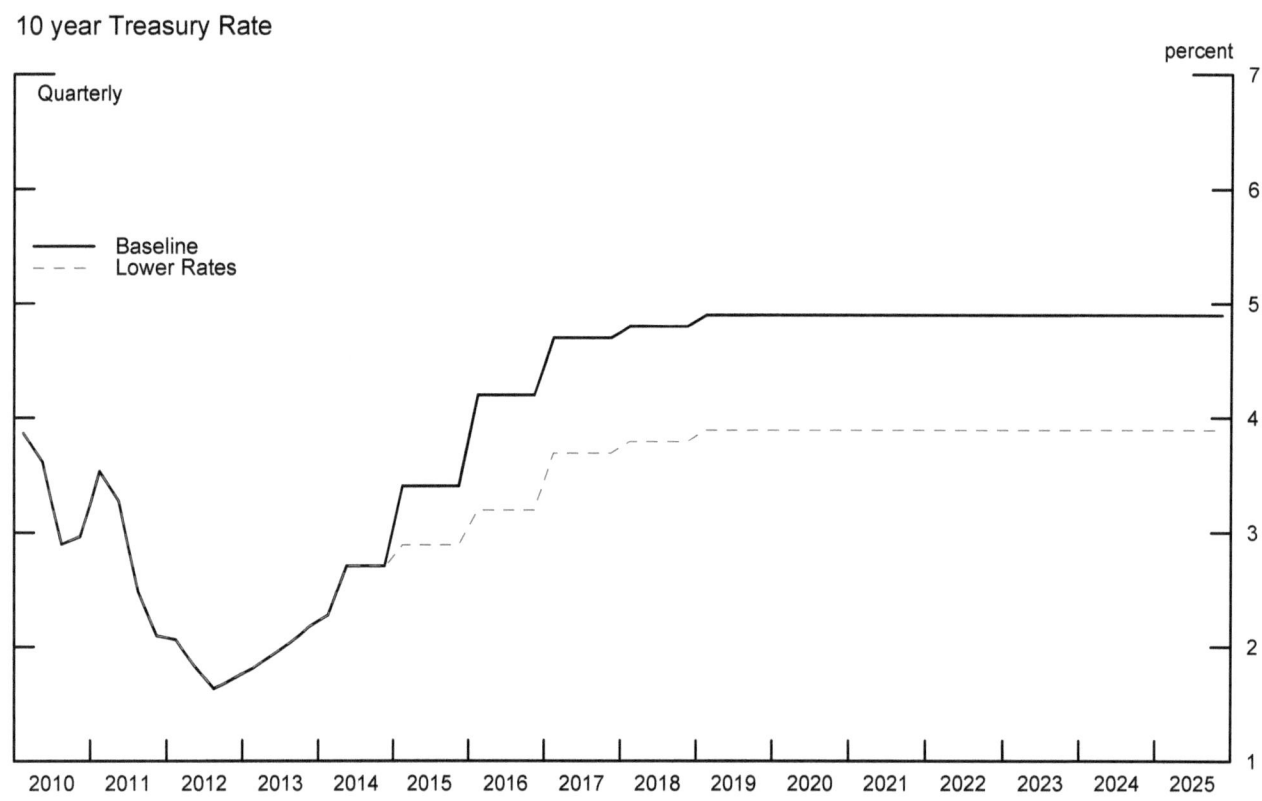

* Baseline interest rate paths are the consensus December 2012 Blue Chip forecast, other interest rate paths are authors' calculations

Figure 16 - Selected Balance Sheet Items with Lower Interest Rates

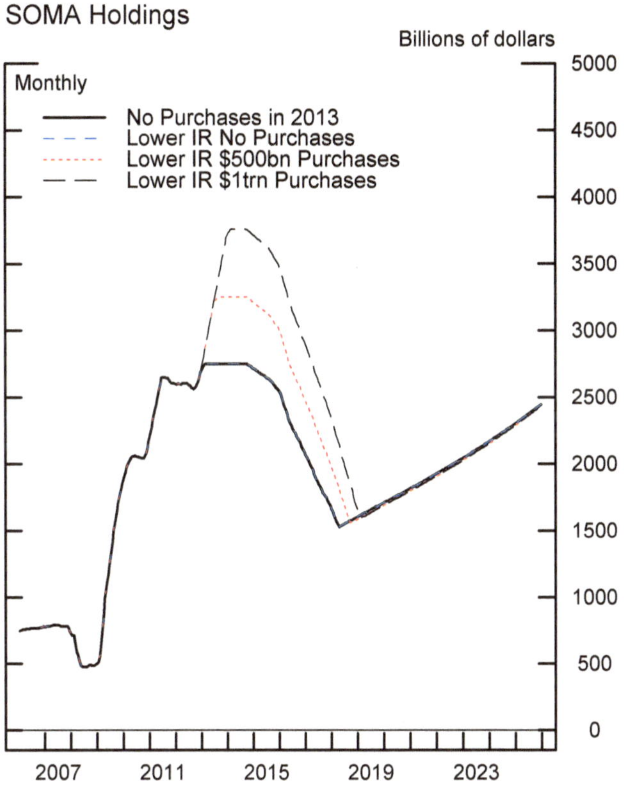

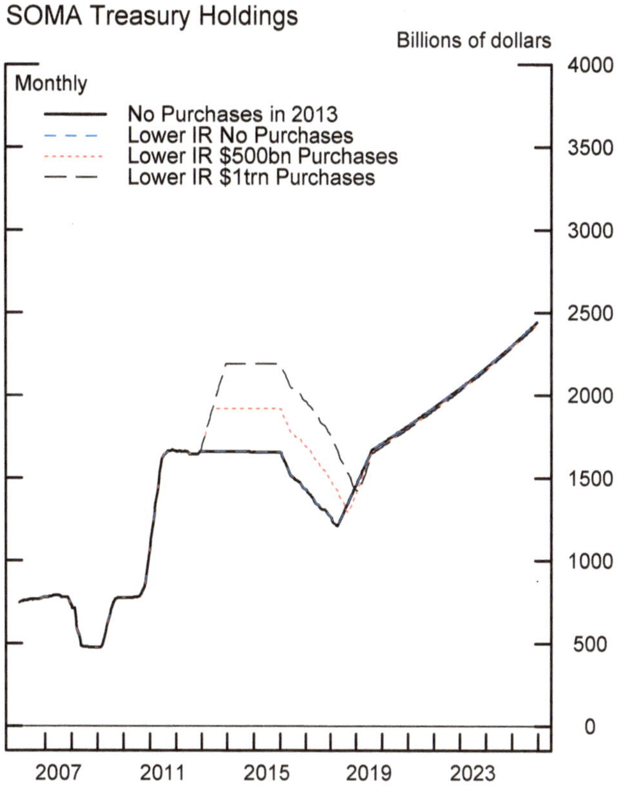

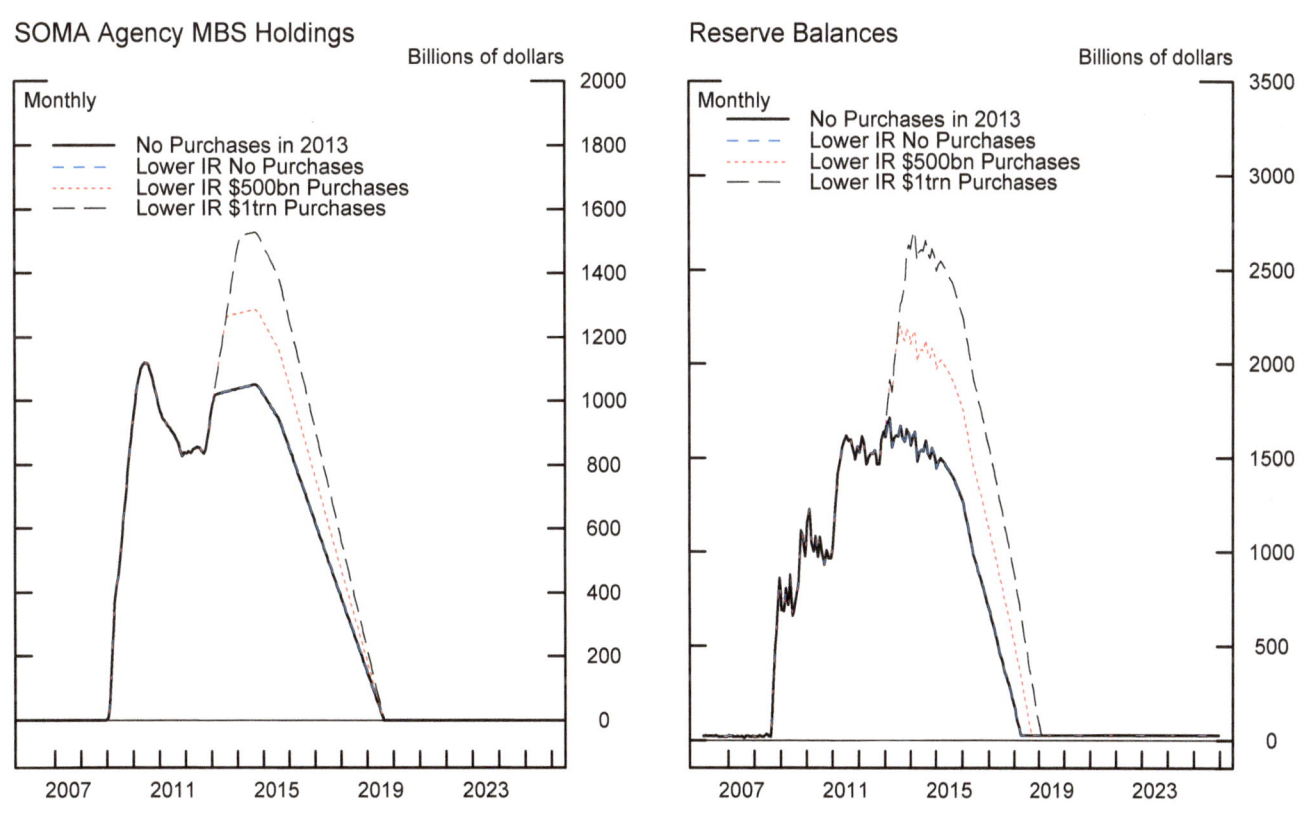

Source: Authors' Projections

Figure 17 - Income Projections with Lower Interest Rates

SOMA Interest Income

Billions of dollars

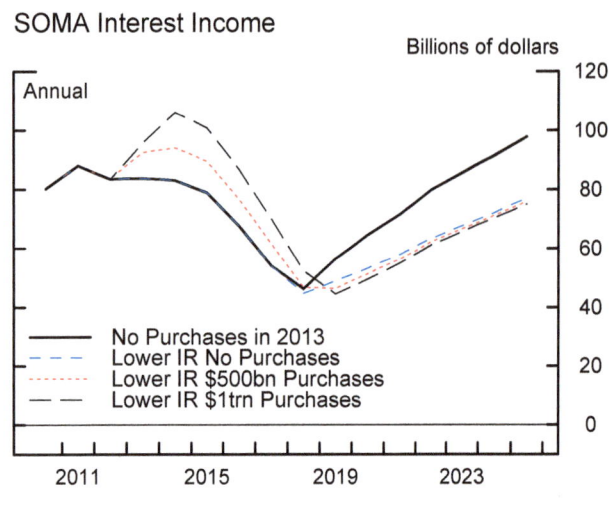

Interest Expense

Billions of dollars

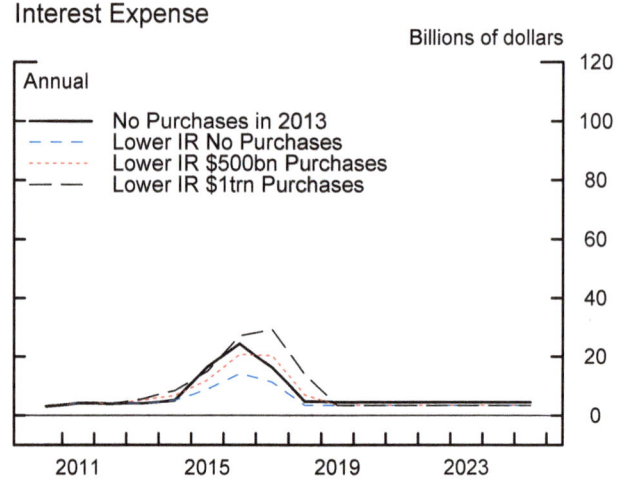

Realized Capital Losses

Billions of dollars

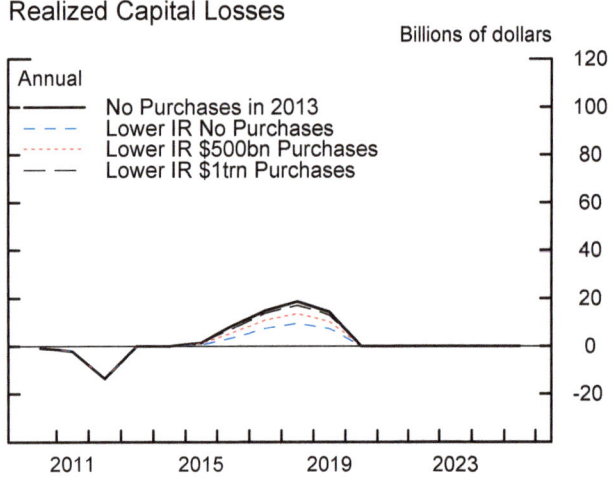

Remittances to Treasury

Billions of dollars

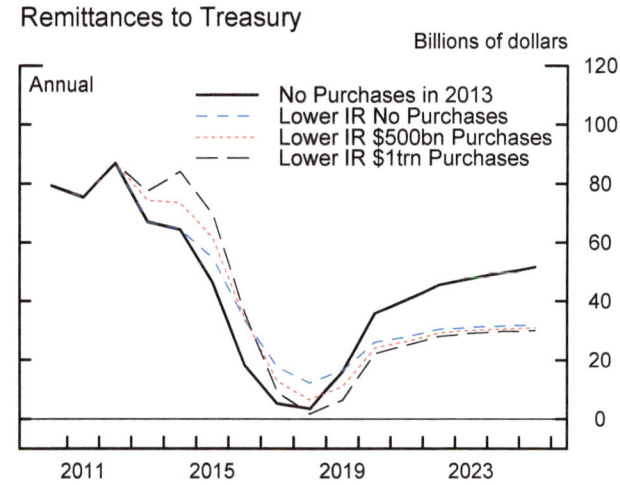

Deferred Asset

Billions of dollars

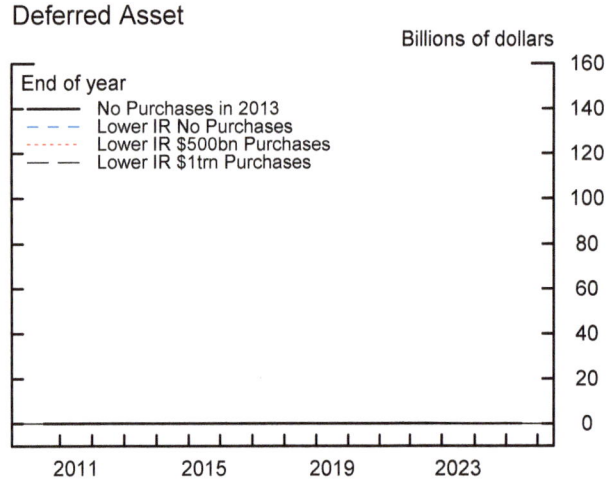

Unrealized Gains/Losses

Billions of dollars

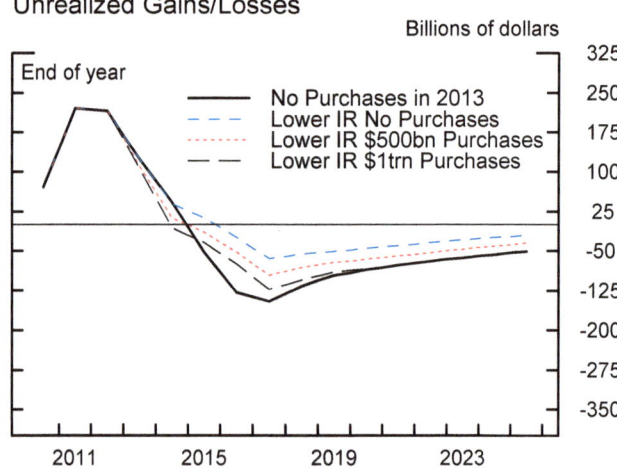

Source: Authors' Projections